The Women's Guide to Consistent Golf

ALSO BY KELLIE STENZEL

The Women's Guide to Golf: A Handbook for Beginners

The Women's Guide to Consistent Golf

KELLIE STENZEL

Thomas Dunne Books
St. Martin's Griffin ☙ *New York*

THOMAS DUNNE BOOKS.
An imprint of St. Martin's Press.

www.stmartins.com

Photos by Anthony Loew
Design by Jessica Shatan

Library of Congress Cataloging-in-Publication Data

Stenzel, Kellie
    The women's guide to consistent golf / Kellie Stenzel.—1st St. Martin's Griffin ed.
        p. cm.
    ISBN 0-312-28230-3 (hc)
    ISBN 0-312-30335-1 (pbk)
    EAN 978-0312-30335-8
    1. Golf for women. I. Title.

  GV966.S75 2004
  796.352'082—dc22   2004041342

First St. Martin's Griffin Edition: May 2004

10 9 8 7 6 5 4 3 2 1

To my father, who is always with me in my heart no matter where I travel. I love you.

To my friends and family for your love and support. I am a lucky girl. I feel blessed.

And especially to my ever-faithful O'Malley.

Contents

Acknowledgments

I would like to thank the members and staff of Atlantic Golf Club. Your support and friendships are appreciated and have been very rewarding. Thanks to my agent, Richard Barber. I have trust and faith in you and your opinions. To Pete Wolverton, my editor, thanks for your helpful comments and your love of the game. Congratulations on being a new daddy. Thanks to Tony Loew for the wonderful photographs. And thanks to the other golf professionals for what I have learned, and will continue to learn, from them. Your sharing of knowledge helps me to be a better teacher every day.

And a special thank-you to Burberry Golf.

Introduction
Being a Consistent Golfer

I've worked with golfers of all skill levels, from a first lesson to a tour player. The most common request is to be more consistent.

To this point, you've been relatively successful at one time or another with each skill: putting, chipping, pitching, sand, fairway woods, and driving. But for some reason you don't seem able to put it all together. On the days that your woods are good, your putting fails you. Or your irons are great and your tee shots are all over the place. Why is this? We have all experienced this: those shining moments when it seems to come together for a few holes in a row, but never seems to last as long as we would like. It never could, because we all would like this consistent golf to last forever. I am not here to tell you that I can teach you to always be consistently perfect. But, with a plan for your golf, as you would apply to your life, you can increase the frequency and duration of your consistent golf.

Think of the successes you have experienced in other areas of your life. Did it just happen out of luck, or did your preparation and hard work get you there? You may have made mistakes along the way, but you learned from them, got back on track, and experienced success.

That is what we will attempt to do here: to give you a business plan for your golf, and to show you what the successfully consistent golfers are doing to prepare themselves for the course, what they see and are thinking and the routines that they run through to get the most out of their golf game.

I have been thrilled with the positive response from *The Women's Guide to Golf: A Handbook for Beginners*. The real reward has been hearing from people I had not previously met, telling me that the book had helped them. I felt that it had really served its purpose to give someone who had never played before a guide to feeling comfortable. On occasion I would hear that the book was so basic that it did not provide enough information for a more advanced student. This was fine, because that was not my original goal. This made me recognize that different levels of ability require different levels of instruction and information. I experience this every day when I teach. For example, I may say the same thing over and over to the same student, but the student will not "hear" what I am saying until she is ready for it. It could even be a year later and the "lightbulb" will go on, and she will say, "Now I know what you mean," with a bright look in her eyes. Now I have said this same thing many times, and in many different ways, but the student has finally reached a level of comprehension or skill that she is ready for the new bit of information.

That is also the goal of this book: to give you a more detailed explanation of your skills, with more advanced options, along with proper decision-making and practice skills to help to increase your consistency. The goal is to help you to make wiser

Introduction Being a Consistent Golfer

decisions by having a specific order with which you approach each area of your golf game.

Men and women are very different, especially in our learning styles. The more I teach, the more I believe this to be true. Women seem to have a strong desire to learn to do things properly the first time. They generally need to know the rules and etiquette, along with the correct way to accomplish each task. Men seem much more likely to just dive right in and figure out the correct form later.

By learning the proper fundamentals and techniques you are more likely to feel comfortable on the range and on the golf course. This is one of my goals: to help you to feel as comfortable and as at home on the range and the golf course as you possibly can.

Your level of comfort will directly affect your actions. When women are not comfortable or do not feel at home, they often get nervous.

My playing partner Peggy summed up how she and many of us can feel when she said, "I would rather give birth in Times Square than play in a golf tournament."

I remember the first time I went to LPGA qualifying school. This is a tournament held once a year for women to attempt to qualify to play on the LPGA tour. I traveled with my friend Jamie to Wichita, Kansas. Jamie is a wonderful golf professional and was formerly the head golf professional at the Thorneblade Country Club in Greenville, South Carolina.

We played our practice rounds and both commented that we were surprised that we were not that nervous. Boy, did that change on the first day of the tournament. As I was getting ready to tee off, five minutes prior to my tee time, I was searching frantically for my yardage book. I could not find it anywhere. Once I started breathing and calmed myself down, I found my yardage book. It was in my mouth! In my mouth! I was out of my comfort zone. So, when you are nervous and uncomfortable with your new surroundings, for example taking your golf skills from the range to the course, or playing with other golfers who may be better than you, or playing for the club championship, I understand how you feel.

If you have relatively solid fundamentals, good decision-making, which provides good course management, and a solid routine, consistent golf is possible.

The amazing thing about golf is that every day is a new adventure. What I experienced golfing yesterday may have nothing to do with my golf today, sometimes for the better and sometimes for the worse.

Your goal, and what I hope to help you with, should be to improve your fundamentals, your routines, and your decision-making. When should you play conservatively and when should you go for it? Practice the techniques mentioned here over time. Your consistency will increase and hopefully so will your enjoyment of the game.

Leftie Apology

This book is written from a right-handed perspective. So, I apologize to the lefties, although I hope it still helps!

The Women's Guide to Consistent Golf

Set Up for Consistent Success

1

If you hope to be consistently successful with your golf, your setup must be solid and the same, or as similar as possible, every time. This is generally the largest difference between low-handicap players and high-handicap players. If your preparation varies from swing to swing, you should expect different results. Focus on your setup fundamentals and you will be amazed at the consistency you can achieve.

Preswing Fundamentals Review

With *The Women's Guide to Golf: A Handbook for Beginners,* I felt it was important to start with the smaller swings and work your way up. I still recommend that you warm yourself up with some smaller swings, pitch shots for example. As you are a more experienced golfer, we will start with a review of full-swing setup fundamentals. The stronger your fundamentals, the more likely you are to have success under pressure.

The fundamentals include grip, ball position, posture, and aim and alignment.

Fundamentals are your building blocks for your golf swing. This is much like the foundation for your house. The stronger the foundation, the more solid the house will be.

Grip

What you must understand about your grip, the position in which you place your hands on the club, is that it controls your club face. The position of your club face will directly affect the direction of your golf ball.

The two goals of your grip are:

1. **The hands are to be positioned on the club as your arms hang.**

2. **You should hold the club in your fingers.**

The Hands Are to Be Positioned on the Club as They Hang When Relaxed

Bend forward from your hip joint and relax your arms by shaking them out. Notice that when you relax your arms and allow them to hang, your palms face toward your body. Now keep in mind that this is very individual. Some of us will have hands that hang more or less turned in than others. This makes the grip a very individual fundamental.

However many knuckles you see on your left hand when it hangs relaxed is the number you should see when you hold the club.

Also relax your right arm and allow it to hang. As you place

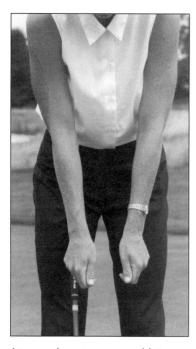  

As you relax your arms and let them hang, your palms face toward your body.

However many knuckles you see on your left hand when it hangs relaxed is the number you should see when you hold the club.

Your right hand should cover the thumb of your left and look as it did when it was hanging.

the right hand on the club, completely covering the thumb of your left hand, it should look exactly as it did when it was hanging.

This is important, and important for you to comprehend, because during your golf swing your arms will return to the position in which they naturally hang.

So, if your hands are on the club other than how they hang, this will directly affect the club face at impact.

This is cause and effect. To possess the skill of self-correction, you must understand how this works.

If either or both of your hands are rotated too far to the right, they will rotate back to the left as you swing, returning to the position in which they naturally hang. This will roll, or

Hands rotated too far to the right.   Hands rotated too far to the left.

close, the club face to the left, tending to make the golf ball go to the left.

If either or both hands are rotated too far to the left, this will roll, or open, the club face to the right during the golf swing as your arms seek the position in which they naturally hang. The open club face will tend to make the golf ball travel too far to the right.

Try this without and with hitting golf balls to help you understand the cause and effect of the grip on the club face.

Rotate your hands too far to the right, then relax your arms. You should see that the club face now aims to your left.

If you have a slicing problem, where the ball curves excessively from left to right, a club face closing would not be a bad thing, would it?

Rotate your hands too far to the right and try hitting a golf ball from a tee. As the club face closes, the ball should fly left, assuming there are not too many other slice issues in your golf swing.

Now try the reverse, without and with hitting the golf ball. Rotate your hands too far to the left and relax your arms. You will see the club face open to the right, tending to promote hitting golf balls to the right.

I wish I had understood this when I was playing the ladies' South African tour with my friend Kathy Hart Wood. She sliced, and I hooked. We would see each other on the tee box and on the green, but rarely in the center of the fairway. Even if the grip was not our problem, changing it could certainly have helped.

Recently I discovered that I was moving my right hand too far to the right during my backswing. This would cause my club face to close and hook the ball severely. This gave me flashbacks to South Africa. I made myself put my right hand on the club correctly, with my thumb left of the center of the grip, and not allow myself to move it. No more hooks! Amazing! I have been playing golf almost all of my life, and I still have to work on my grip.

Not Comfortable

Now don't think that this change feels good to me. It feels terrible! But it works! My golf ball likes it. Therefore, no matter how wrong it feels to me, I am committed to making this change.

When I worked for Mike Adams, a fabulous golf instructor from whom I learned a lot, he would always say, "Do not confuse comfort with correct." This makes a lot of sense.

The crease between your fingers and your palm of your left hand should rest on the side of the club.

The heel pad of the left hand should rest on the top of the grip.

You should be able to balance the club between the index finger and the heel pad of your left hand.

The Club Should Be Held in the Fingers

As you place your hands on the club for your full swing, you should hold the club in your fingers. This will allow you to have control without tension and will allow the wrists to hinge properly. Both of these will help to promote distance.

Place your left hand on the club so the crease between your fingers and your palm rests on the side of the club. Remember to relax your arm and allow it to hang as you do this. As you close the hand around the grip, the heel pad of the hand should rest on the top of the grip. This will hold the club in place, requiring little pressure to keep the club in position. If the club is properly held in the fingers of your left hand, you should be able to balance the club between the heel pad and the index finger. This allows you to simply close your hand around the club, rather than needing to squeeze, and helps to promote club-head speed and distance.

Your Glove May Give You Away

If you are holding the club incorrectly in the palm, the club will slide around in your hand throughout your swing, often leaving a wear mark or eventually a hole in the heel of your golf glove. So, although you thought that glove was defective and returned it to the shop, maybe it wasn't the glove.

As you place your right hand on the club, be sure to completely cover the thumb of your left hand, so that your right thumb rests just left of the center of the grip.

Other Signs You May Be Holding the Club Too Much in the Palm

Generally, I see that women who hold the golf club incorrectly in their palms hit their golf ball short and to the right.

The Lightning-Rod Swing

When the club is held in the palms, the increased tension necessary to keep the club from sliding inhibits the wrists from hinging properly. With this grip, the club often points straight at the sky on the backswing or the forward swing, or often both. This loss of leverage decreases speed and therefore distance.

Try to snap a towel using only your shoulder (one lever and less power) versus your shoulder and your wrist (two levers and more power).

Erect Posture

A golf club held incorrectly in your palm will cause you to stand too upright, so that your rear end will appear tucked under, with your spine too upright and your knees probably overflexed. This will put you in an out-of-balance, nonathletic position, making you less efficient.

Try It Both Ways

Practice holding the club in your palms and then in your fingers. Make small circles with the club head out in front of your body, so that you can feel how much easier it is for you to allow your wrists to react freely to the weight in the club head when you hold the club in the fingers rather than the palms. Holding the club properly in the fingers allows your hands to react naturally to the club head and makes it much easier to achieve consistent results.

The "Swoosh" Advantage

The club held in the fingers will help you to make that nice swoosh noise that sounds so nice and helps to promote distance. We will talk more about this later.

Holy cow! That is enough about the grip already. Pretty important stuff, though.

Ball Position

Ball position is one of your most important fundamentals, because it can affect all the others.

Short Irons

For your sand wedge through your 4 iron, the golf ball should be positioned just left of the center of your stance. The golf club should be centered in your body; therefore the ball would be just ahead, or left, of the club head.

Proper ball positions—short irons, centered; long irons and fairway woods, just left of center; and driver or teed woods, left instep.

Long Irons and Fairway Woods

For your long irons, 3, 2, or 1, if you are brave enough or crazy enough to carry them, and your fairway woods—those woods you would use to hit a ball from off the ground without a tee—the ball should be placed just slightly farther left than for your short irons, or approximately in the front third of your stance.

Long Irons, Who Needs Them?

I used to carry a 2 iron. I used to love it, but technology has improved, and I do not have the time to practice and play as much as I used to.

About four years ago, my good friend Terri Norris, a wonderful instructor in San Antonio, Texas, sent me a generous gift of a 9 wood. Very nice of her, but when I received the club, I wasn't sure if I would ever use it. So, I carried it around with me for a few weeks without ever taking it out of my golf bag. One day while playing at Atlantic Golf Club in Bridgehampton, Long Island, where I have the privilege to teach in the summer, I was struggling with my long irons, so I decided to break out the good old 9 wood Terri had sent to me. What the heck, at this point I didn't have anything to lose. It was a nice par 3. I took a couple of practice swings, then hit this beautiful, straight shot right onto the green. It was just so much easier, and so much more fun, than the low, excessively curving shots I was hitting with my long irons. I not only still love my 9 wood, but have since added a 7 wood and taken my 2 and 3 irons out of my golf bag. And I don't miss them either.

Why This Works

The more loft a golf club has, the more backspin it will produce, which gives the golf ball lift. The more club-head speed you generate, which varies person to person, the more backspin and lift is produced. This is why Tiger Woods hits the ball so much higher and farther than you or I do. He generates so much more club-head speed he needs no help to get the ball into the air. If anything, he wants the opposite. He may wish to keep his ball flight lower to have better control.

This is the same concept as an airplane needing a certain amount of speed for takeoff.

The higher-numbered fairway woods have built-in loft relative to the long irons, therefore helping the lower-club-head-speed player, such as many women, myself included, get the ball into the air with less side spin. Higher and straighter works for me!

Many of the Tour Players Are Doing It!

Annika Sorenstam has traded in her long irons for higher-numbered fairway woods, as many of the other players have. The number of long irons on the LPGA tour has drastically decreased as the number of fairway woods has increased. If you have not tried a 7 wood or a 9 wood, you should. They should make it easier for you to hit the ball consistently straighter.

What Is Best for You?

In my opinion, unless you carry your 5 iron more than 150 yards, you should experience more success with higher-numbered fairway woods. (Hitting a 5 iron 150 yards equates to a driving distance of more than 220 yards, which a relatively low percentage of women golfers achieve.)

Ball Position for Your Driver or for Teed Woods

Your ball position for your driver or teed fairway woods should be just left of that for your long irons or fairway woods. In other words, the ball should be in line with the instep of your left heel, or your left shoulder socket. You will position the ball left in your stance because the ball is on the tee, helping you to catch the ball slightly on the upswing of the semicircle of your golf swing.

Help in Finding Proper Ball Position: Start with Your Feet Together

To help you to find a proper ball position, start with your feet together (touching) and then step each foot appropriately, always stepping left foot first. Running through a routine such as this can make it easier to always have proper ball position, which is a wonderful step toward being a consistent ball striker.

Short irons: Step each foot equidistantly.

Long irons and fairway woods: Step your left foot slightly less than your right.

Ball-position routine for a short iron—start with your feet together. Step your left and right foot equidistantly.

Driver or teed woods: Step your left foot only slightly, approximately one to one-and-a-half inches, then step your right foot the rest of the width of your stance.

I have found this helpful because when you start with your feet together, it is easier to position your golf ball in the center of your body to start, then adjust from there.

On the Course—Make It Work!

Now you know where your ball should be positioned in your stance; however, the game of golf is not that cut-and-dried. The

To avoid "popping up" your tee shots, your left shoulder should be higher than your right because your left hand is higher on the grip than the right.

dreaded curveball: You are on the course and you keep hitting the ball fat, ground before the ball, and you can't figure out the problem. Make it work! Survive the round with your sanity intact. Put the ball where you are hitting the ground. So if you are hitting the ball fat, move the ball more to the right in your stance where you are presently hitting the ground. This will hopefully help you make it through the round until you can get to the range or your golf professional to discover the root cause of your problem.

Popping Up Your Tee Shots

Check your ball position, and quick! Is it getting too centered? If your ball position drifts too far back in your stance when your ball is on the tee, this could cause you to catch the ball too much on the downswing and pop the ball up. Understand, the angle at which the club contacts the ball is the angle the ball will come off the club. Be sure to play the ball more toward your left instep.

You may also want to check that your shoulders are set properly, so that your left shoulder is slightly higher than your right, simply because your left hand is higher on the grip than your right. This would directly affect the angle that the club contacts the ball.

Tee It Higher, Not Lower

Now I know your Prince Charming just told you to tee lower when you popped up your last tee shot, but don't listen to him! The lower you tee the ball, the more you will force yourself to go down to get the ball, producing a steeper angle of attack, therefore more pop-ups.

Tee the ball higher and learn to sweep the ball off the tee. You should never take a divot with a tee shot.

The angle at which your golf club comes into the golf ball is the angle at which the golf ball will come off the club. So, if you chop into the ball, like the letter V, the ball will fly high and short. I love to see the top of the tee just slightly clipped for any wood from off a tee.

Posture

Correct posture will allow you to be balanced in an athletic position. Being in balance at address and throughout your golf swing will make you more efficient, and therefore more consistently successful.

Correct posture for golf means you'll be bent forward from your hip joint, so the chest is over your toes. This will allow you to maintain a straight spine. It is important that you differentiate between your hip joint, which is correct, and your waist, which would be incorrect.

Correct posture: Bend forward from your hips, with your chest over your toes, so that your hands can hang directly below your shoulders. Notice that your knees are only slightly flexed.

Your spine should be straight from your head to your tailbone.

Practice bending forward from your hips by keeping the shaft of your club against your spine, resting from your head all the way to your tailbone as you bend forward. If you are bending forward correctly, you will feel as if your rear end is sticking out. Yes, I said your rear end sticking out. I know you have been taught the opposite for most other aspects of your life.

Lessons Well Learned

Growing up, I had a gymnastics coach who was well endowed, and she would always say, "If you've got it, flaunt it," and I guess this is one of those cases. This is also the same woman, Marty, who would make us do fifty push-ups if we said the word *can't*. To this day I remember her lessons, and I continue her tradition with my junior golfers in an attempt to rid their vocabulary of the word *can't*.

As you bend forward from your hip joint, allow your arms to relax and hang, so that your hands hang directly below your shoulders. You should feel your weight in the balls of your feet.

Just a Little Knee Flex

Flex your knees enough to simply relax and take the lock out of your legs. Your hip joint, not your knees, is your lowerer. You should be able to see clearly all of your shoelaces.

If you overflex your knees, your rear end tucks under too much, your upper body becomes too erect, and your weight settles too far toward your heels. In this case, you will surely be out of balance.

Stance Width

Your heels should be approximately hip width apart for all of your irons, and slightly wider for your woods. The widest your heels should ever be is shoulder width.

How Do You Know If Your Stance Is the Right Width?

Measure the width of your hips from hip-bone to hipbone using the rubber grip on

Your heels should be hip width for your irons and slightly wider for your woods.

your club. You can use this as a measuring stick for your feet. Check this periodically to consistently have proper stance width.

What Happens If Your Stance Gets Too Wide?
If your stance gets too wide, you will tend to have too much lateral motion as your weight attempts to transfer naturally. This is generally about the time your Prince Charming tells you that you're swaying. Fix the cause—that is, narrow your stance—and you will fix your problem.

Aim and Alignment

You will aim your club face, then align your body. This must occur in this order, so that you build your setup around your club face. To aim consistently well, you will need proper concepts, a good routine, and efficient practice.

Aim your club face to the target and build your setup around your club face. Notice that the club and hands are set before you set the feet.

Aiming the Club Face

You should aim your club face to your target so that the scoring lines on the club face are perpendicular to your target line. Most golf clubs are designed well today, so that if you let them sit flat on their bottom, they will set relatively squarely.

Aligning Your Body

Once you have aimed your club face to your target, you should align your body so that the lines across your heels, hips, and shoulders are parallel to your target line. So, your body lines are parallel to the target line, but slightly left relative to your target. In other words, the lines across your heels, hips, and shoulders should aim slightly left of your target.

Align your body so that the lines across your heels, hips, and shoulders are parallel to your target line. These lines aim slightly left of your target.

Most Righties Aim Too Far Right

Most right-handed players, myself included, aim too far to the right. We forget to set our body lines slightly left of our targets.

To help with this, be sure to keep your left shoulder out of your line of sight to your target. In other words, you should never look over your left shoulder at your target, but rather inside the shoulder.

Alignment Must Be Practiced

My friend and colleague Jeff Warne coauthored a book with Phil Lee titled *Shrink Your Handicap.* My favorite chapter in the book stresses that alignment must be practiced, as must any fundamental, to be reinforced.

Yes, Miquette, There Is a Santa Claus

One of my students, Miquette, convinced herself she could not align properly. I like her very much, as a person and as a student, and she challenged me to explain alignment to her in as many ways as I could come up with. And I think that I came up with a lot. She has dramatically improved as her concept has improved. Hopefully, Santa Claus will bring me the right words, so she will completely understand.

Why the Fundamentals Are and Will Continue to Be Your Keys to Success

You've been successful, at one time or another, with each of these skills required to play golf. Now, you're wishing for more consistent success, be it for a full round of golf or a competitive endeavor, such as the ladies-member guest or the club championship.

The more solid your fundamentals—grip, ball position, posture, and aim and alignment—the more likely they are to hold up in pressure situations. It could be teeing off in front of your friends or needing to get the ball up and down from the bunker to win your club-championship match on the eighteenth hole in front of the clubhouse. The more solid your fundamentals, the more likely you will be to play consistently well throughout your entire round.

In golf, two wrongs can make a right. These two wrongs require good timing. The more pressure, the more your timing will be challenged. And this is why under pressure golf swings can fall apart and make you inconsistent.

Take a Minute!

Ask yourself, are your fundamentals strong enough to hold up under pressure? And when they start to break down, are you able to recognize the early signs of the problem? To be a more consistently successful golfer, you must recognize the signs of an oncoming problem.

The Tour Players Are Working on the Same Things

The best players in the world work to improve the same areas in their setup as the average golfer, but simply with a greater eye for detail. Your setup and your fundamentals absolutely shape your golf swing.

I watched a video golf lesson in which Juli Inkster took a lesson from Mike McGetrick. This was before her amazing run of wins that she has amassed over the last couple of years. All that she and Mike worked on was her setup. They worked on nothing complicated, just fundamentals.

Setup Station—for Productive Practice for Consistency

1. When you practice, are you productive?

2. Do you practice to a specific target?

3. Do you use an alignment aid when you practice?

If you can answer yes to questions two and three, you are more likely to be able to answer yes to question one.

If you wish to transfer your good shots from the range to the golf course, practicing correctly is a great help.

Rick Jensen, a sports psychologist whom I had the privilege to work with at PGA National, often speaks of a study conducted at TPC Sawgrass in Jacksonville, Florida. The PGA tour holds the Tour Champion-ship there every year. The study compared the practice habits of the average golfer versus those of the tour player. The week before the tournament, while the resort guests were playing the course, the study kept count of the number of alignment clubs or aids that were used in practice. It totaled approximately five for the entire week. Then the tour players arrived. Their total for the week exceeded two hundred alignment aids. Theirs was quality practice. Productive practice leads to more on-course consistency.

For the small amount of time required to lay an alignment club on the ground and to have a specific target, the long-term benefits are well worth the effort.

Your alignment and ball position should be practiced by using a setup station.

Setup Station

Your setup station should include at least one alignment club, but preferably two. Place the two clubs on the ground parallel to each other, so that the line down the center of them points to the target. Be sure to point the club heads out and behind the ball to avoid injury. If you need to check your ball position, you can also place a club perpendicular to your alignment club that will rest between your feet.

2
Practicing: When You Have the Time, Have a Plan

At some point you need to pay your dues and put in your practice time. I don't mean that you need to quit your job or put your children into day care for the rest of their lives. But, a small bit of practice time with specific quality goals in mind can go a long way.

You and Your Golf Professional Are a Team

If your practice is to be productive, you must be working on proper fundamentals. Your professional is a small but necessary part of your golf. You cannot see yourself, and even if you could, do you possess the technical knowledge to diagnose the cause of your problem? This is where the trust and confidence you and your professional share will come into play.

I want my students to know that I am there for them. I am part of their support system. A student will often approach me and say, "Can you watch me hit a couple of balls? I am struggling. And I know that you can fix it in five minutes." With many of my students whom I have worked with over time, I can put them back on the right track quickly. In other cases, the problem may be more involved and may require a concession to help the student get through an upcoming round, before a formal lesson later.

Repetition with Feedback

Rick Jensen tells a story of how Nick Price wore out the faces of three 9 irons making one change in his golf swing. For the change to become habit and to work under pressure, he had to put in his practice time.

Watch the better players at your club. As a general rule, their practice habits are pretty good. It seems that the lower handicappers spend a higher percentage of their practice time on their short games. And I do recognize the feeling of needing to get there (or around the green with the ball generally getting airborne) first, before you need to worry about your short game.

One of my students, Mariana, has done well. We were on the golf course playing and she was on the green of a par 5 in three shots. She then four-putted. At this point we had to put things into perspective. I said to her, "It took three shots to travel four hundred and sixty yards, and that's great, but it took you four more from thirty feet." Mariana gave me a guilty look, and she still reminds me of that story. It is not that her putting stroke has any major mechanical problems, but she just hadn't practiced enough to develop her feel. Her putting has since improved with a little practice. I can teach you mechanics, but you have to earn feel.

The Bruce Lietzke Types

Bruce Lietzke, a PGA Tour player, is known for how well he plays even though he rarely practices. He plays fewer tournaments than many of the other tour players. He is lucky, number one, because most of us do not have this luxury. And number two, I commend him because he places his family at such a high priority that he limits his travel schedule. And although he does not have the most orthodox swing, he is consistent in his results because he repeats his setup and his individualist swing over and over.

Club Professional Makes Cut at U.S. Open at Pebble Beach

Rick Hartmann, whom I work with, is the head golf professional at Atlantic Golf Club in Bridgehampton, New York, and a fantastically talented player. This past summer (2001), not only did he qualify for the U.S. Open at Pebble Beach, but he made the cut. It was an amazing accomplishment and fun to watch. The members were so proud and excited. Now, Rick is not a big practicer. He will hit a few balls here and there and roll a couple of putts once in a while. He does have the advantage of playing in quite a few tournaments, and he plays with the members regularly. What you don't see is how much he used to practice. He put in his time. He has hit the balls and practiced the putting when he attempted to play for a living. He has achieved an elite level of golf. So, what we see now is not a lack of practice, but quality practice and maintenance. Congratulations, Rick!

A Realistic Practice Schedule

Let's assume, like most people, you are overscheduled. That life thing can certainly get in the way of a golf game. Here is a suggestion for a basic practice schedule that is complete and efficient.

The time frame is one month. You will need to take three one-half-hour lessons, accompanied by six one-hour practice sessions. So, your total time investment is seven and one-half hours of practice per month. Quality practice will be stressed. Now that's not so bad, is it? Feel free to increase practice or lesson time if you so desire. If you are not willing or able to put in the six hours of practice to supplement your three half-hour lessons, you should increase your length and frequency of lessons.

Example of a One-Month Lesson and Practice Schedule

Day 1: a half-hour lesson; a half hour to practice what you worked on in the lesson; a half-hour practice on your short game—one and a half hours total.

Day 4: practice a half hour on full swing; practice a half hour on short game—one hour total.

Day 9: a half hour lesson; a half hour to work on changes; a half hour on short game—one and a half hours total.

Day 12: practice a half hour on full swing; practice a half hour on short game—one hour total.

Day 17: a half-hour lesson; a half hour to practice what you worked on in the lesson; a half hour on short game—one and a half hours total.

Day 25: practice a half hour on full swing; practice a half hour on short game—one hour total.

Feel free to spread the lessons and practice sessions out as is convenient for you. If you are unable to get to a practice facility this often, you can develop an at-home program as well.

Setting Goals and How to Practice

How do you get the most out of your committed seven and a half hours of lessons and practice? The first step is your golf lesson. Your lesson should be a running dialogue, and a team effort between you and your professional.

You will need to communicate to your professional any problems you may be having, and what your desired result would be.

Your professional must be able to communicate the cause of your difficulty in a manner that you can understand, and what changes you will need to make to accomplish a correction.

Not only should you listen intently to the necessary changes, but you should write them down at the end of your lesson. Also, consider repeating them back to your professional at the end of the lesson to clarify any confusions you may have. Your goal for each lesson should be to understand what you need to change for improvement.

The Half Hour Following Your Lesson

Start with a five-minute break. This will give a little time to rest, get a drink, or just to clear your head for a minute. During your half hour of practice, your only goal should be to reinforce what you worked on in your golf lesson. If you have been assigned a practice drill to assist you in making the correction, this is the time to do it.

Do Not Let the Ball Be Your Master

This is easier said than done, but important for you to understand. Always, always keep in mind your goal. This is one thing the golf professional will always be better at than you. Stay focused on your goal, not each ball's results.

For example, if you and your professional are working to rid you of your slice by strengthening your left-hand grip, and you hook the ball during practice, that is a good thing. Let yourself make the opposite mistake. The opposite mistake is good. I said that three times on purpose. Say it out loud. The opposite mistake is a good thing.

Short-Game Practice

You know you should practice your short game. This is the quickest way to shave strokes from your score. The more consistent your short game, the more it will take the pressure off your long game. The less pressure on your long game, the more likely it will be consistent under stress.

This is an example of a quick and efficient short-game practice schedule that I put together for one of my students, Ellen. The better you become, the less time this will take. With a little practice, you should be able to finish in approximately fifteen minutes.

Each goal is a quality goal. The sooner you accomplish each goal, the quicker you will finish.

1. *Putting:* three-footer monorail drill. Sink ten three-footers in a row.

2. *Putting:* two-putt drill. Putt between two cups, back and forth, with only one golf ball. Your goal is to two-putt or better ten times in a row.

3. *Chipping:* Choose a generic chip shot where you have room for one-third carry and two-thirds roll, where you will use your pitching wedge. Your goal is to chip eight out of ten balls within a three-foot circle of the hole.

4. *Pitching:* Choose a generic pitch shot where you need equal amounts of carry and roll. Your goal is to pitch seven out of ten balls within a four-foot circle of the hole.

As soon as you accomplish each goal, you should move on to the next. The more proficient you become in each area, the quicker you will finish. This is a quick and efficient way to hit each area of the short game. And now you have no excuse for not knowing what or how to practice.

Playing Golf with Others and Feeling Comfortable

This is an issue that we all have to deal with at one time or another.

One of the first tournaments I played in as a junior golfer was the Finger Lakes Championship at Corning Country Club in Corning, New York. This is a beautiful course, which also hosts an annual LPGA event. With my newly established 32 handicap, and a severe case of nerves, I went through my normal warm-up. I hit golf balls to warm up my full swing, then rolled some putts on the putting green. As I was hitting a few chips from the side of the green, I missed one quite badly. It scooted across the green, close but not threateningly so to one of the other women. She then predicted that I and my playing partners were in for a long day. This threw me for a loop, and then I found out I was paired with her. I did have a long day, because I was not prepared to deal with this. I will try to help you to deal with these situations.

Watch and Learn from Better Players

Look at playing with better golfers as an opportunity to learn from them. Do not necessarily learn their individual golf swings, but how they handle themselves on the course, how they manage their shots, and how they save shots relative to your game.

The wonderful group of ladies who took me under their wing as I was growing up taught me a lot. I would arrive at the green much sooner because I could hit the ball longer than they. They would still beat me with their short games. I learned by watching and learning from their experience.

Play Your Own Game

It is not necessary to keep up with the Joneses. You should play your normal golf game. An attempt to be heroic often ends in collapse and disappointment. If you press to hit the ball farther or attempt risks you would ordinarily not, you'll most often fail. Keep in mind that the A player in your group does not expect or necessarily want you as a C player to play as well as she. The A player generally expects to do most of the work. If you help here and there, you have more than contributed your fair share.

A woman where I used to work, named Judy, is a wonderful golfer and has been for a long time. The higher handicappers are scared to death of her. A pairing with Judy in an ABCD tournament will often send the B, C, and D golfers into near-death stress. That is until they make it past the first couple holes. Judy is actually supportive and nice to play with. Many of the women would come to me afterward in surprise to say they enjoyed their day. A sheep may be dressed in wolf's clothing. Keep in mind, however, the reverse can also be true.

The Chameleon Effect

We all have our own atmosphere of comfort when it comes to our golf. You may like to talk while you play, or you may prefer a quieter, concentrating golf game. You may be a speed demon or a more methodical planner.

While you should understand and maintain your basic style of golf, even when you are playing with lower-handicapped golfers, you may need to adjust your style to accord with the better player's. This is called the chameleon effect. Your better player will generally set the pace and the atmosphere for your round, and you must learn to adjust your game within reason.

Observe and Adjust

The first step to finding a complementary atmosphere is to observe your fellow golfers. Play your own game and watch the others for the first few holes. If their style is similar to yours, today is your lucky day! Just relax and enjoy it. Be sure to get names and phone numbers for future games with these golfers.

If their style is very different from yours, you must attempt to find a happy medium. For example, if the better player does not like to talk, and you do, you must respect her style. But there are plenty of ways to handle this. You can be less talkative and speak more with the other golfers. You can talk to yourself—I've done this. Or you can sing. Singing is a wonderful way to keep yourself calm and play within your style, as a talker.

Dealing with the Rude

It is going to happen, so be prepared. At some point you will be paired with a player who is rude.

Several suggestions for playing with rude players:

1. Limit your conversation with that person. Rude players often make negative remarks. Try to be polite and answer any questions as simply and succinctly as possible. Avoid falling into negative or complaining conversations with them.

2. Arrive early for your tee time. If you arrive early, you'll more likely be able to ride in a cart with another player in your group.

3. Rather than dwelling on the negative vibes coming from Ms. Rude, focus on something positive in your surroundings. Maybe this should be the day you notice all of the wonderful work your golf superintendent does for you and your golf course.

Being comfortable will allow you to play good golf with a player who is better. You may have heard that playing with better players helps you to elevate your own game. I agree, but only if that person is positive and supportive.

I have played with several PGA tour players who are friends of mine. That they are friends allows me to be completely comfortable with my game, since I am comfortable with them as individuals. Yet to play with a tour player whom I don't know would be a different story. Therefore, if possible, choose the better players you play with wisely.

Breathe and Focus

To control your nerves, be sure to breathe. I know this sounds pretty elementary, but controlling your breathing can also help you to lower your heart rate. Focus on your target and yourself. These are the things you have control of, not the other players in your group.

Taking Lessons

In my opinion, my friend Jeff Warne said it best: "Your instructor and your lessons are a small but necessary part of the equation."

The higher level of golf you play, the more important it is that you choose an instructor with a proven track record. Who are the best instructors in your area? Ask the better players at your club where they take their lessons. Now, I am not suggesting that you make a change if you are improving your game with your present instructor. If something is working, do not change; if it isn't broken, don't fix it. However, if you feel you have applied yourself and you're not seeing improvement, a different perspective can be good.

Putting: Never Three-Putt Again

3

To be a consistent putter, your setup and fundamentals must repeat. You must also have quality practice that stresses distance control.

Setup and Fundamentals Review

Setup

1. *Grip:* Your grip for putting will vary from that of your full swing in that the palms should face each other, rather than opposing. Your thumbs should point straight down the center of the shaft. You'll notice that most putter grips have a flat topside of the grip to accommodate this.

2. *Ball position:* As you clap your hands together, they meet in the center of your body. This is where you should

position your putter. As your putter sits centered in your body, the golf ball will sit just left of center. Centering the putter in your body can simplify the task of keeping all of your body lines parallel to the target line. Note: You will often see golfers who position their golf ball slightly farther left in their stance. This can be acceptable, provided that the golfer's shoulder line is parallel to the target line. Your arms and therefore your putter will swing down your shoulder line.

You should center your putter in your body.

3. *Posture:* Bend forward from your hip joint. If you do so correctly, this will position your chest over your toes, while your spine remains relatively straight. You should bend your knees only enough to take the lock out, and relax your legs. If you overflex your knees, your posture is too upright and unathletic.

Your putting posture: Bend forward from your hips so that your eyes are over the ball and your hands hang below your shoulders.

Posture Checkpoints

Your eyes should be directly over the golf ball as you bend forward from your hips. This will help you to see the target from a truer perspective. You can check this in a mirror, or by dropping a golf ball held close to your eyes, to see that it lands on your golf ball on the ground.

Your hands should hang directly below your shoulders. As you bend forward from your hips, so that your chest is over your toes, you should relax your arms and allow them to hang, perpendicular to the ground. This will promote a proper path, as well as allow you to separate your upper body from your lower body. Isolating the upper body will help you to make the correct stroking motion.

Stroke Motion

Arms and shoulders: Maintain the triangle. In your putting stroke, move only the triangle formed by your arms and across your shoulders, as only your upper body generates momentum. Your lower body should not move. Your wrists should maintain their angles and be solid throughout your stroke.

You Think You Are Staying Still, But You Probably Are Not

One of my students, Linda, told me she was struggling with her putting. I watched her several times on the practice green, and everything looked fine. So, out to the golf course we went. She was correct. She was really struggling. But on the course she was totally different. Her lower body was moving so much that it looked as if she were taking her full swing. We made two adjustments. First, we set her up pigeon-toed, which helped to restrict her lower body from moving. Second, we made sure she completed her stroke before she turned her head to see the ball rolling. Both of these adjustments helped to keep her lower body steady, increasing her ability to control her distance and make her shorter putts.

Same Length Back and Through

When you putt, your stroke must be the same length back and through. This will help you to maintain an even tempo and make it easier for you to control your distance.

Your stroke should maintain the triangle formed by your arms and be the same length back and through.

Practice Techniques for Consistency

To be a consistent putter you need to do two things:

1. Control distance.

2. Make a three-footer.

My college coach at Furman University, Mic Potter, would tell our team that most double bogeys end with a three-putt. Most of the time, he was right. I have played many respectable rounds where I did not hit the ball well, but I have never played a good round where I putted poorly.

When you are preparing for a tournament, I suggest you increase your time on the practice green.

Distance Control

Once you feel that your stroke is fundamentally solid, most of your practice time should focus on distance control, aka feel. You can be taught fundamentals, but your level of feel will fall upon your shoulders. You need to pay your dues on the putting green.

First, to get a general feel for the speed of the greens, hit several medium to longer putts. Move around the green, so you are stroking different putts, uphill, downhill, left to right, and right to left. Continue moving around the green until you have been relatively successful at putting the ball close to the hole. If you do not reach this point, then keep going. The more putts you roll, the more feedback you have.

Tempo

Consistent putting requires a tempo that is continuous throughout, much like that of a pendulum. To maintain a consistent tempo, use the same grip pressure throughout your stroke. Take time and practice this.

How to Adjust for Putts Continually Short of the Target

If your putts are always coming up short of your target, you should first check that your stroke is the same length forward as it was back. If you incorrectly abbreviate your forward stroke, the ball will often end up short of the target.

You can use the three-tee drill to check this. Place three tees in the ground in a line, so that the outside tees are of equal distance from the center tee. The ball should be placed in line with the center tee. Stroke the putt so that your putter head travels even with the back tee, then through to the forward tee. Hold your finish to check that you have accomplished the goal of being the same length back and through. You could also at this point check to see that the back of your left hand has gone to the target, and that you have maintained your wrist angles.

The second fundamental to check if your putts are continually coming up short is the length of your stroke. If your back stroke is too short, it will be difficult to get the ball to the hole, no matter what type of forward stroke you make. Increase the length of your backstroke, and therefore your forward stroke as well.

I recently had the privilege to travel to Kiawah Island in South Carolina with members from Southampton Golf Club who were celebrating their club's seventy-fifth anniversary. On the course that we played the first day, the greens were slow. The three ladies whom I was playing with, Nancy, Donna, and Donna, all came up short on their first putts. They were all used to relatively quick greens, therefore their backstrokes were way too short compared to what they needed. Since they were all my teammates, I urged them to greatly increase the length of their backstroke to get the ball to the hole. Several times they commented that they needed to hit putts harder, but this was not the case. They needed more stored energy provided by a longer backstroke. Fortunately, they increased their stroke sizes, got the ball to the hole, and our team did quite well.

A Trick

If your putts continually come up short, aim to a point past the cup. Aiming at a point past your target can help convince you to take a longer stroke.

How to Adjust for Putts Continually Long of the Target

If your putts are continually rolling past the hole, check the following fundamentals:

Too large of a backstroke would generate too much power and most often produce a putt that rolls too far. Shorten the length of the backstroke and your forward stroke will produce less energy and not roll the ball as far.

Hitting, rather than stroking, your putts will often roll the ball too far. Your tempo and grip pressure should stay consistent throughout your stroke. If you force your forward stroke, aka the hand-explosion putt, which is often accompanied by an increase in grip pressure, the ball will often roll too far.

Focus on keeping your tempo even. You might notice when you start to stroke your putts rather than hit them that the sound of the ball coming off the putter face is different, not quite as loud. Focus on keeping your grip pressure even, rather than ever grabbing or pulling the putter.

Too much body motion often produces a putt that rolls too far. A steady lower body will increase consistency in both distance and direction. If your lower body moves during your stroke, your weight may transfer slightly and produce excess distance. Focus on freezing your lower body, so that you see zero movement in your knees. You may also want to double-check that you are bent forward from your hip joint, rather than your waist, which makes it easier to isolate your upper body from your lower body.

Tricks to Hitting Putts a Shorter Distance

1. Look short of the hole. By focusing and aiming at this spot short of the hole, you can trick your eyes into seeing a shorter putt. This is often a good technique for a downhill putt. This is a system we used at the Academy of Golf at PGA National, under the direction of Mike Adams.

2. Place your hands lower on your putter grip. By placing your hands lower, you in essence make the putter shorter, which shortens the lever and therefore produces less energy. Once again, this is often a good technique for downhill putts, or very fast greens.

Think like a Professional: A Putting Routine That Works Under Pressure

Now that your practice putting sessions have prepared you for on-course pressure situations, it is time to check your on-course preparation and decision-making. Your preparation, better known as your routine, is your script for success in consistency. Watch the better golfers you play with. Their preparation routines are often so ritualized that they can take on a personality of their own.

A fellow teammate and a good friend of mine from Furman University, Kristin, recently visited me in Florida. Even though I had not played golf with her in about seven years, her routine and idiosyncrasies had not changed in the least. We all have our own individual little movements. This individuality makes my job different and interesting every day. Keep in mind that no one routine works for everyone. The following example is to help you understand what low-handicap or professional golfers are thinking and doing before they stroke the ball.

1. Read the Green

The first step is to read the green to calculate how the ball will break, and how any changes in elevation will affect the speed of the putt.

You'll want to start by getting the big picture. Start to read the green as you approach it. Every green will have a predominant tilt to promote drainage. Look for the high side of the entire green versus the low side. It is much easier to see the predominant fall of the green versus the subtle undulations that you will need to assess next.

Once you have read the big picture and are on the green approaching your ball, start to get a feel for any hills or slopes on the green. Use both your eyes and your feet.

As you stand behind your golf ball, so that it is between you and the cup, compare the left side of the putting line with the right side, up to about three to four feet on either side. Often I find it difficult to just look at the line and read the putt. But if you compare side to side, it is often much easier to see the lay of the green.

You can also look at the cut of the cup in the green. There may be a slight tilt, with one side higher than the other, which will clue you in to the amount of slope.

I like to look at the cup as it sets in the green, because hopefully at this point the ball will be slowing down, with gravity affecting it more. This is why the break of the ball generally increases as it approaches the end of its rolling. Always expect the slope of the green to curve the ball more toward the end of the putt than at the beginning.

For example, I may have a putt that breaks in two directions: left to right for the first half, and right to left for the second half. Although the undulations may look the same to me, I would generally aim the ball slightly more to the right because that is the way the green falls through the second half.

As you read the green for side-to-side breaks, you will also want to have a feel for uphill versus downhill. Looking at the whole green, or the big picture, can also be helpful with this.

2. Pick Your Aim Spot—Putt to an Imaginary Cup

Once you have read your putt to make an educated guess as to the direction it will break, and the lay of the green, being uphill or downhill, you will want to pick a spot at which to aim. You must disregard the actual cup and aim for this spot.

If the green is higher on the right side of the cup, I would then pick a spot to the right of the actual cup. If the left side is higher my spot would be to the left of the cup. The more dramatic the slope, the more I would favor the higher side.

So, this takes care of the side to side, but what about the uphill and downhill?

If you have a downhill putt, which will increase the speed at which the ball rolls, you want to aim for a spot that is short of the cup. If you have an uphill putt, you should aim for a spot past the cup. This system helps your eyes to trick your body into adjusting for the slope of the green.

Let's put these two ideas together so you can pick one spot to aim. Should you have a downhill putt that curves from right to left, your aim spot, or imaginary cup, should be short and right of the actual cup. In this case, I may slightly increase the amount I aim to the right because the putt is downhill, which generally increases the amount the ball breaks.

For a downhill, right-to-left putt, your aim spot should be short and right of the cup.

Another example: If I have an uphill putt that breaks left to right, my aim spot would be left and beyond the cup. Beyond the cup addresses the uphill, and left addresses the break.

Once you choose your aim spot, this becomes your target. You should be focusing on the spot, not the cup.

One of my talented students, Roz, was struggling with her putting. Her fundamentals were fairly solid and she was able to read the greens pretty successfully. Once she set up, aligning to her aim spot, she would look right at the actual cup, abandon her aim spot, and always miss the putt on the low side of the break. Once she began focusing on her aim spot and kept that as her target, she had a lot more success.

Tips for Picking Your Aim Spot

1. **Right side of the green higher than the left—pick a spot to the right of the cup.**

2. **Left side of the green higher than the right—pick a spot to the left of the cup.**

3. **Downhill—pick a spot short of the cup.**

4. **Uphill—pick a spot past the cup.**

5. **Downhill—increase the amount of break you will play for.**

6. **Uphill—decrease the amount of break you will play for.**

3. Practice Stroke or Strokes Looking at Your Target

Your next step is to take your practice stroke or strokes looking at your target, which is the aim spot. Your goal is to take in the distance information visually, and for that reason you should be looking at the target, rather than your feet or the putter head. If you have never done this before, and many golfers do not, it will feel and look strange at first.

Watch the golfers on television. As they take their practice strokes, they are most often looking at their target to have a feel for the distance.

I take tennis lessons. I love tennis. I am still learning and improving. I also believe this helps my teaching golf, because I experience lessons from the student's perspective. My tennis professionals, Brenda and Mike, explained the split step to me. As your opponent hits the tennis ball, you should make a split step, landing on each foot simultaneously to prepare for your next shot. I had never done this before nor noticed that it occurred. As I watched tennis on television that weekend, I saw that the pros all did this. I was so unaware to that point. I learned a lot from watching the professionals on television, once I knew what to look for.

A feel for the distance will help you to determine the size of the stroke you will take. This should be the goal of your practice stroke: to determine the size of the stroke you will take. Therefore, your practice strokes should completely mimic what you hope to do when the ball is struck.

4. Set Up to Putt

So, you have read the green, picked your aim spot, and taken your practice stroke. Now it is time to set up to stroke the putt.

The first step in setting up is to aim your putter face to your target (aim spot, don't forget!). The most successful routine, in my opinion, is to set your putter to the ball while aiming the face, then to build your setup around your putter. In other words, set the putter, then set yourself. The line on the putter, if there is one, should point to the aim spot, so that the putter face sets perpendicular to your target line.

Once you have aimed your putter face to your target, you will want to set yourself to your putter. As you continue to look at your target, set your body so its lines (feet, hips, knees, shoulders, and eyes) set parallel to your target line.

Once you feel set, you should take one last look to your target, checking that you feel comfortable with your alignments.

5. Complete Your Stroke, Then Turn Your Head

You are all set to go. Your actual stroke should mimic your practice stroke. Be sure to complete your stroke before you turn your head. This will help to ensure your lower body remains steady until your stroke is complete.

In Summary

Now, this probably seems a lengthy process, but in reality it occurs quickly:

1. Read the green.

2. Pick the aim spot.

3. Take your practice stroke looking at the target.

4. Set up by aiming your putter face and then aligning yourself.

5. Make your stroke while remaining steady.

Your Routine Should Repeat

To be consistent on the course, your routine should be virtually the same with every putt, not only in what you do, but in the order and the tempo in which you do it. As you improve, even the little details of your routine will repeat, down to the number of practice strokes you take or the number of times you look up to the target throughout your routine.

Quality Goals for Consistency

Practice for Distance-Control Consistency

Once you have a general feel for the speed of the green, you will want as realistic a situation on the practice green as possible to that on the golf course. This requires setting quality goals, which will produce the same level of pressure and importance on your putting as you would experience on the course. Quality goals, rather than quantity goals, increase your on-course consistency—the ultimate goal!

For example, if my goal is to roll ten forty-footers within a three-foot circle of the cup, this might be good practice, but there is little pressure. It may take me fifteen, twenty, or thirty tries, but it is quite simple. But, what if my goal is to roll five forty-footers within a three-foot circle of the hole in a row? Big difference! Because, what happens when you get to number five? The fifth putt has pressure and consequences if you do not succeed. You have to start all over. This is now a very different experience. You now have the same pressure and accountability you experience every day on the golf course.

Quality-oriented distance-control practice techniques include:

Attempt to roll your longer putts within three feet of the cup.

1. As above, designate a distance and a number of putts in a row that you need to roll within three feet of the hole. You can measure three feet easily, as it is probably just longer than the length of your putter. Place tees

in a circle around the hole to help you to recognize the successful putts more easily.

2. My favorite drill is to pick two holes on the putting green and to putt back and forth. Set a quality goal of a certain number of putts or better in a row needed, before you can stop. For example, I may pick two cups on a slope so I experience uphill and downhill on every other putt. My goal is to two-putt or better ten times in a row. This helps you learn to adjust your stroke size for the same length putt, uphill versus downhill. This is not always as simple as it sounds. I have seen players who thought they were relatively good really struggle to complete this goal. Once you feel relatively successful with two simple cups, challenge yourself with either a longer distance between the two cups, or two cups with more severe breaks in the green.

3. Putt to increments of ten feet—ten, twenty, thirty, and forty feet. Place a tee in the green from which you will putt. Place tees in the green at ten-foot increments. You can measure this by taking three and one-third large steps. One large step, based upon the length of your legs, is about one yard, or three feet. Alternate putting to each distance. Once again, set a quality goal to make your session on the practice green resemble what you will experience on the course. Try to putt twelve balls in a row within three feet of each distance. That twelfth putt will have the pressure you experience on the course. If that putt is not within three feet, you will have to start all over.

Now that you are able to roll the ball within three feet of the hole consistently and under pressure, all you need is to be able to make a three-footer. If you can accomplish these two goals, you'll never three-putt again, right? Well, less often, hopefully.

While working on your three-footers, you should also work on the mechanics of your stroke. The more mechanically sound your setup and stroke, the more likely you are to be consistent in your results.

Three-Footer Mechanical Check

Use the monorail system to check your setup and the path of your stroke. Place one of your irons on the ground just outside of your golf ball so that an extension of the shaft points to the right edge of the cup. The monorail system will allow for the slight semicircular motion of the stroke as it elongates. It may not be very noticeable on your shorter putts.

As you address the ball, the club on the ground will assist you in double-checking your setup. First, you should check to see that your putter face is aligned at a right angle or perpendicular to the shaft on the ground.

I realize this sounds very basic, but putter-face misalignment is one of the most common reasons I see many of my students miss short putts. I often aim my putter face too far to the right, so when I practice using the monorail, my putter face often looks to be aiming farther left than normal, but I know it is correct.

I like to see all the body lines, including feet, knees, hips, shoulders, and eyes, parallel to the target line and a monorail club. The most important of all of these is the shoulders, since the arms will generally swing down your shoulder line. Using the club on the ground, you can check that these alignments are parallel. Using your alignment aid

The three-footer monorail drill.

will help you to set up properly throughout your practice time so you don't waste time practicing bad habits.

Now that you have checked your putter-face and body alignments, you can check the path of your stroke. Your putter head should move relatively parallel to the monorail club, with some semicircular motion acceptable. The putter head should never cross the monorail club. If the putter head crosses the monorail, the club face delivers a glancing blow to the ball, leading to inconsistency in distance and direction.

Stroke a number of putts next to the monorail checking your setup and fundamentals. You should also check that the length of your stroke is the same back and through.

When you are feeling relatively comfortable with your stroke, you should return to quality goals to mimic the conditions you'll experience on the golf course. The more your practice sessions can mirror on-course situations, the more consistency you will experience.

Three-Footer Quality Goals

Attempt to make a specific number of three-footers in a row, for example twenty. If you miss a putt, you should start again at one. As you get to the teens, you will experience the pressure you can expect every day on the golf course.

If you find this task is too easy, either increase your targeted number of consecutively made putts or increase your distance to four-footers.

Adjusting to Different Greens

You are scheduled to play in the ladies-member guest down the street. You can bet that the greens will not be like those you are used to. And yes, this may sound like a good excuse for the first couple of greens. But last that I looked, the scorecard had no place set aside for excuses.

If you do care about your score at the end of the round, you must prepare yourself before the round.

You should definitely spend time on the putting green before your round. In my opinion you should spend two-thirds of your warm-up time on the practice green and the rest warming up your swing.

To be more specific, start your warm-up on the putting green. Your goal should be to get a good feel for the speed of the greens; therefore, I recommend you hit a lot of medium-large to large putts. Work your way around the green, stroking uphill, downhill, and side-hill putts that break in both directions. You should feel free to hit a few short putts, but don't waste too much time on them. Should you miss them, you are only undermining your confidence. Keep in mind, should you truly expect to make these short putts, you should be going through your full routine. I feel the time is better spent hitting longer putts so you have a better sense for the overall green speed.

You may find it helpful to compare the greens to those you are used to. For example, these may be just a little faster or slower. The more dramatic the difference, the more time you will want to spend before your round.

When you start to feel relatively comfortable with the green speed, go to the range and warm up your full swing. This should be a warm-up, not a practice session. Start with your shorter clubs and work your way up to the club you will tee off with.

Once this is complete, and you have a feel for how you are hitting the ball that day, return to the putting green to stroke a few last putts.

This is the quickest way to save strokes when you play a new golf course.

What If You Do Not Take the Time to Warm Up Properly?

You are on the first tee at the ladies-member guest down the street from your club, and you forgot to warm up your putting on the practice green. What should you look for to help you determine the speed of the greens?

1. Really fast greens almost shine. They will give off more of a gray-green color, rather than bright green. This is because, with the grass cut so short, the blades are relatively small. If this is the case, I strongly suggest your aim spot should be quite a bit short of the actual cup.

2. Slower greens will generally look shaggy like a carpet, often with large blades of grass. If you look at the cups and a lot of thick blades are overhanging the edges, you should assume that the greens are slower. Remember in this case to aim past the cup.

With no warm-up time, you'll have to go with your visual cues on your first putts.

Left-Hand-Low Putting

The popularity of the left-hand-low putting style has dramatically increased. It may be worth trying if you struggle with your stroke.

You should reverse your hands so that your left hand is set lower on the putter grip. You should also set your ball slightly farther left in your stance, since the bottom of the arc occurs later, due to the left hand being lower on the putter.

This setup helps minimize or eliminate the flipping or breaking down of the wrists.

You can also use this style as a practice aid to help you feel your wrists maintaining their position throughout the stroke.

My brother, Rob, could hit the ball quite well, but his putting left something to be desired. After reading an article in the magazine *Golf for Women,* he decided to try left-hand-low putting, with dramatic improvement.

Left-hand-low putting setup.

Short Game

4

Your short game is a key to overall consistency in your golf. Some days you will hit the ball better than others; that is a given. When your short game is solid, you can save a lot of strokes and still score well on those days when you do not hit the ball as well. Also, proper shot selection, choosing the highest-percentage shot for the situation at hand, will help to decrease the penalty for mishit shots and will increase your consistency.

Shot Selection: To Chip or to Pitch?

To quickly review:

> **A chip is generally lower in flight, with less air time and more roll time.**

A pitch is generally higher in flight, with more air time and less roll time.

You will need to determine whether you can chip the ball or need to pitch it.

Step one: Assess the lie. Do you still have both options available to you?

Step two: As the lie worsens, the more limited you will be. The worse the lie, the less the chances that you will be able to loft the ball into the air.

You need to understand that as the lie gets worse—for example, the ball may be sitting down in deep rough—the more necessary it will be for you to move the ball back in your stance, or toward your right foot. Moving the ball back in your stance will help you to catch the ball more on the downswing, so that all that rough will not stop your club before it gets to the ball. That is the good news. The bad news is that the more you move the ball back in your stance, the more the loft of your club face decreases. So, the priority of extracting the ball from the poor lie takes precedence over lofting the ball over any obstruction, such as a bunker or long grass. The worse the lie, the fewer your options.

Play the Percentages

Every short-game shot you have gives you another choice as to the highest-percentage (safest) shot possible. This leads to higher levels of consistency.

1. **Putt whenever you can. Putting is the highest-percentage shot, with the lowest chance for disaster or embarrassment. A bad putt will always be better than a bad chip or a bad pitch. If your golf ball is off the putting green, but**

on reasonably short, flat grass, you should still seriously consider putting.

For example, Atlantic Golf Club, designed by Rees Jones, a wonderful architect and a nice person, has a lot of "spillways" that run off the back or the sides of the green. The grass on the slopes is closely mown and nicely manicured. Although it would probably not be your first inclination, the best option is to putt, even though the hill is relatively steep. Just try it!

2. If you can't putt, your next best option is to chip. The chip, having less air time and more roll time, is your second-best, and more forgiving, option. Because a higher amount of the total distance of the shot is roll, a smaller stroke is needed. The smaller the stroke, the less the chance of error. Many times, a slightly skulled or thin chip shot can end up just as good as one hit properly.

3. If you cannot putt or chip the ball, you'll have to pitch. Because the bulk of the distance of the shot will be in the air, you'll need a larger swing. The larger the swing, the greater the chance of error. Should you mishit a pitch shot, the results are often quite penalizing due to the larger swing.

Review:

1. Putt if you can.

2. Chip if you can't putt.

3. Pitch only if you have to.

My father always taught me to try to miss the ball as straight as possible. That is the basic premise for this system as well. The more playable your misses, the more successful you will be. This often depends directly on intelligent shot selection.

Chipping

Generally hit from around the edges of the green, a chip shot will have less air time and more roll time. Since the ball is rolling for a majority of the distance, the size of the required stroke is smaller. The smaller the swing, the less the chance of error. Therefore, chipping is relatively low on the embarrassment scale. So, we like chipping. Often, a bad chip and a good chip have similar results.

When to Chip—Less Ground to Carry and More Green to Work With

Assuming that you are too far off the green to putt, when the distance of your golf ball to the edge of the putting surface is less than the distance from the edge of the green to the cup, you should chip.

When You Can Land the Ball Short of the Green and Let It Run Up

If the approach area short of the green is relatively flat and manicured, you should feel comfortable landing the ball short and letting the ball roll up. The lower you keep the flight of the ball, rather than throwing the ball into the air with a pitch shot, the more you are in control.

Setup and Fundamentals Review for Chipping

Grip down and step in: To put yourself more in control, you should place your hands lower on the grip. Feel free to go close to the bottom of the grip of the club. On your very small chips, I even recommend you set part of your right hand below the bot-

For chipping, you should place your hands lower on the grip and step in.

Your stance should be narrow with your forward foot pulled slightly back. Notice that your weight and the handle of the club lean left.

tom of the rubber grip and on the shaft. Anytime you grip down on the club, it will be necessary for you to step in closer toward the ball to maintain posture and balance. The more you grip down on the club, the easier it will be for you to have consistent results due to increased relaxed control.

Stance narrow with left foot slightly pulled back: Your stance should be relatively narrow, which will help to avoid too much body motion. I like to see the heels no wider than about six inches apart.

Your left foot should be slightly pulled back, but no farther than the toe of your left foot in line with the ball of your right foot. This will help you to keep your weight on your left foot throughout the stroke. Be careful not to pull your left foot back so far that it opens your shoulders excessively so that they are no longer parallel to the target line. I do not want you to look as if you have been to too many chipping clinics. I often see students who are so twisted and discombobulated from swinging the forward foot around, or even the entire body, that any sense of direction is nearly impossible. When this occurs, the ball rarely travels to the target. So, pulling your left foot back slightly means *slightly.*

Ball position: Here is where you will have some options. As you become more advanced, you can use your imagination to produce your desired results. Your ball for chipping should be either centered or slightly back in your stance. Since your stance is not excessively wide, we are probably talking about three to five inches of options. It is important that you understand how the ball position will affect the flight of the golf ball. The farther back you position the ball in your stance, or toward your right foot, the lower the trajectory of the ball coming off the club face, and therefore the greater the roll. The more centered your golf ball in your stance, the higher the flight. To remember this, think "right foot for roll." The more I want the ball to roll, the farther back in my stance I will position the ball.

If you are playing golf and the greens are slow and your chips keep coming up short, place your ball farther back in your stance. This will increase the percentage of roll and offset the slow pace of the greens.

Weight stays left: Your weight should favor your left foot about 70 to 30 percent and remain there throughout your stroke. This helps to eliminate too many moving parts, making you more consistent with your distance and direction.

Shaft leans left: The shaft of the club will angle slightly to the left toward the target. This is partially because your weight is favoring your left foot and will be accentuated the more you play the ball toward your right foot.

Setup made simple: With all that you have to remember about the chipping setup, it can seem overwhelming. Yet with a simple

Chipping setup made simple. Start with your feet together with the handle pointing to the center of your body. As you step your left foot left, allow your weight and the handle to move left also.

and efficient setup routine, you can get set up perfectly with ease. Start by gripping down on the club and place your feet together so that they are touching and the ball is centered. Take your left foot and step it left toward the target and slightly back so that the toe of your left foot lines up with the instep of your right. As you step left, allow your weight to move left and the handle of the club to lean left in line with your left pocket. With one simple step you are in a perfect chipping setup that will help you to maintain a consistent ball position with all of your chips. Be careful to maintain the alignment of the club face as it loses loft when you lean the handle left.

Just like a putt that sweeps the grass: Now that you are set up properly, it is time to learn the stroke. The chipping motion is similar to that of a putt and involves mostly the arms and the shoulders with minimal lower-body motion. The bottom of your club will sweep the grass. This will provide the ball with enough air time to carry any longer grass that may be between you and your landing area. That there are fewer moving parts when chipping aids its being more consistent.

Same length back and through: Similar to the pendulum motion in putting, the chipping stroke should be the same length back and through. The energy in should equal the energy out.

Descending angle of attack: Because your weight favors your left foot, your back stroke should feel a little more upright or steeper, and the forward stroke will come out lower to the ground. This is the result of the slight shoulder tilt produced by your weight being on your left foot throughout the stroke.

Flat left wrist at impact and beyond: The angle that you start with or create in your backstroke should be maintained throughout your forward stroke. There should be no flipping of the hands on the forward stroke.

Often instructors teach chipping with no wrist movement at all in the stroke, myself included. But after reading an article by Jim McLean in *Golf* magazine, and watching some videos of tour

The chipping stroke should be the same length back and through. Notice the flat left wrist at impact, and that as the club sweeps the grass, the ball travels into the air.

players chipping, I see many of them slightly hinge their wrists in their backstrokes, then maintain that position on their forward strokes.

All good chippers have a flat left wrist at impact, and whatever angle the right wrist attains in the backstroke should be maintained throughout the forward stroke. This is a fundamental that I constantly see Todd Anderson at The Breakers working on with his students. I have been fortunate to work with him, and his professional demeanor and knowledge set an example that all instructors could learn from, as I have.

Club Selection

Your club selection for chipping will allow you to use your imagination and express your individuality to produce different results. The more lofted the club you select—a sand wedge for example—the less roll you will get. The lower-lofted clubs will produce a higher percentage of roll.

If you were to land the ball on a relatively flat green of medium speed, you should expect approximately the following percentages of carry versus roll. Your ball position is assumed to be in line with the big toe on your right foot.

Sand wedge = $^1/_2$ carry and $^1/_2$ roll
Pitching wedge = $^1/_3$ carry and $^2/_3$ roll
9 iron = $^1/_4$ carry and $^3/_4$ roll
8 iron = $^1/_5$ carry and $^4/_5$ roll
7 iron = $^1/_6$ carry and $^5/_6$ roll
6 iron = $^1/_7$ carry and $^6/_7$ roll
5 iron = $^1/_8$ carry and $^7/_8$ roll

The higher the amount of roll you need, the less lofted a club you will use. The advantage to you here, once again, is that the smaller the swing you take, the less the chance of error. The less the chance of error, the greater your consistency.

Trajectory and Roll-Percentage Controllers

1. Club selection

2. Ball position

3. Amount of shaft angle forward

When I teach a newer golfer chipping, I generally recommend one ball position for all of her chips. I will also recommend that she use only two clubs, the pitching wedge and the 7 iron for example. You would use the pitching wedge when you needed slightly more roll than carry, and the 7 iron when you needed a high percentage of roll. As you become more experienced, the sky is the limit on your options. The combination of different clubs and changing your ball position will give you the ability to control your golf ball better through trajectory and roll.

Not Always Just One Right Club

You are in a chipping situation, just off the edge of the green, needing approximately one-quarter carry to the edge of the green, and three-quarters roll to the pin. What club should you use? What are your options? Which options would tend to be more consistent?

Although some clubs may be better than others, there isn't necessarily one right answer. Let's look at the options and see what might work.

Sand wedge: Chipping with your sand wedge will produce approximately one-half carry and one-half roll. This would require you to take a larger swing to land the ball half the distance to the target. This larger swing makes this choice less attractive.

Pitching wedge: Your pitching wedge will give you one-third carry and two-thirds of roll. If you move the golf ball farther back in your stance, you will receive more roll. This might work, especially if you tend to hit your chips too far, or if the greens are quicker than those you are used to.

9 iron: Your 9 iron will give you approximately one-quarter carry and three-quarters roll. This fits this situation. This will allow you to land the ball just on the green and roll it the remainder of the distance to the target. This would allow you to take a smaller swing, which is lower risk and more consistent.

8 iron: Your 8 iron will give you one-fifth carry and four-fifths roll when the ball is positioned in line with your big toe on your right foot. If you were to hit the ball from here, it would tend to roll too far. You might use this if you were tending to come up too short, or the greens were particularly slow. Another option is to move your ball into a more centered position, which would slightly increase the effective loft in the face.

7 iron: Your 7 iron will give you one-sixth carry and five-sixths roll. For this situation, this is too much roll. Even should you center your ball position, this is still too much roll, producing a shot that will travel too far. So for this situation, a 7 iron or any club less in loft will roll the ball too far and not work.

So for this situation you have three options:

a pitching wedge with the ball farther back in your stance;

a 9 iron with the ball in line with the big toe on your right foot; or

an 8 iron with the ball more centered in your stance.

Your choice is based upon your preferences. The more advanced you become, the more options you'll have to produce success.

To help you to understand this, move the ball position in your stance while maintaining the aim of the face. You should see that as your ball position changes, so does the loft in the face. When you center the ball, you will have the actual loft of the club. The more you move the ball back in your stance, the more the loft is decreased and the percentage of roll increased.

Understand this:

Sand wedge with ball back in your stance = pitching wedge with ball centered in your stance

Pitching wedge with ball back in your stance = 9 iron with ball centered in your stance

9 iron with ball back in your stance = 8 iron with ball centered in your stance

8 iron with ball back in your stance = 7 iron with ball centered in your stance

Ball position directly influences the effective loft in the club face. The more you move the ball back in your stance, the lower the ball will travel and the more it will roll.

Think like a Professional: A Chipping Routine That Works Under Pressure

Your decision-making, preparation, and sequence of performance will determine your level of success and consistency. What are the lower handicappers and professionals doing differently from those of lesser abilities? The following will help you answer that.

1. Assess the situation to determine whether you should chip. Your golf ball is relatively close to the green, let's say within approximately twenty yards. First you should decide that you are not able to putt—because of an obstacle or the grass is too long. Chipping is your second choice where you have less ground to carry than green to work with, or where it is okay to land the ball short of the green or on the fringe and allow the ball to roll the rest of the distance.

2. Select the appropriate club and the landing spot. The first step in choosing the correct club is to assess the lie. The worse the lie, the more you'll want to position your golf ball back in your stance. This will help you to catch the golf ball more on the downswing and hopefully before all the grass can twist or affect the club face. The more you move the ball back in your stance, the more you decrease the effective loft of the club.

   The next step in choosing the club is to determine the nearest point to you, preferably relatively flat and manicured, where you can land the ball. Pick the closest spot available because this will allow you to take the smallest stroke. Once again, the smaller the stroke, the less the chance of error.

   Once you have chosen your landing spot, you will want to estimate the distance from your golf ball to that spot relative to the distance from that landing spot to the target. If you determine that one-quarter of the total distance is to the landing spot and three-quarters is from there to the target, you would choose a 9 iron. You do not need to memorize the percentage for every club if you can remember that the sand wedge is one-half carry and one-half roll. As you go to pitching wedge, then the 9 iron, etc., the basic denominator changes to one-third, one-quarter, etc.

3. Next, take your practice stroke or strokes while looking at your target, which is the landing spot. You want to be looking at the target during your practice stroke to ensure you have a good visual feel for the carry distance. Practice strokes should mimic the one you will actually take with the ball. This should include the same setup, stroke size, and tempo. The purpose of this rehearsal stroke is to determine what size stroke you will make, so that during the actual stroke you are repeating something that you have just felt rather than having a new experience.

4. Now that you have chosen your landing area and your club and taken your practice stroke, it is time to pull the trigger. As in your putting routine, your first step in setting up is to aim the club face to the target, then set your body to the club. Remember to grip down and step in, and your ball position should be centered to back based upon the lie or desired trajectory. Your stance should be narrow with your left foot pulled slightly back. Your weight should be favoring your left and stay there throughout your stroke so that your club shaft should angle slightly forward toward the target. Once you completely set up, take one last look to your target, look back at your golf ball, and make the stroke. Your actual stroke

should be an effort to repeat exactly what you have rehearsed in your practice strokes.

Practice Techniques for Consistent Chipping

Chipping 101

I want you to choose a generic chip shot and hit it over and over until you feel successful not only with your distance control, but also the direction. Find a spot just off the edge of the green, where

Set quality goals. Practice chipping within a four-foot circle of the hole.

you have a relatively good lie, that will give you one-third of your distance to your landing area and two-thirds for roll to the target. This will require a pitching wedge. Repeat the shot until you have a strong sense of the size and tempo of the stroke necessary for success.

Once you have a good feel for the desired motion, switch to a quality goal. Quality goals will help you to increase your consistency on the course. By applying meaning and pressure to your practice session, you are better prepared to handle the same pressure you will experience on the golf course, when it does count.

For example, your quality goal may be to chip nine out of ten balls within a four-foot circle of the hole. Now, you can't stop your practice until you accomplish this goal. So, what happens when you get to the eighth ball and you've already missed one? Now you have the pressure that you experience every day on the golf course. You are practicing with purpose, and with accountability for your actions.

If your goal is too easily accomplished, increase the difficulty.

One Club to Different Targets

Choose one club and practice chipping to different targets. This will help you to learn to control your distance by varying the size of your stroke.

So, let's say you decide to practice chipping with your sand wedge, which will generally be half carry and half roll. If the green is relatively flat, attempt to land your golf ball halfway to the target. If the green is uphill, you should land the ball past halfway; downhill, land it short of halfway to accommodate the slope.

Make your preparation mimic what you would do on the golf course. Be sure to take your practice strokes looking at your landing spot, which in this case is halfway to the cup.

Once you are feeling relatively successful chipping to different targets with the same club, switch to a quality goal to help you increase your on-course consistency. An example would be to chip eight balls in a row within four feet of alternating holes. This helps you to learn to adjust your stroke for varying distances, as will be necessary on the golf course.

When doing this drill, you may find that the sand wedge works better to some targets than to others. This will also help you to understand how the ball reacts and help you with on-course club selection.

Vary the club that you choose for this drill, so that you practice with all of your clubs over time. If you choose a club with lesser loft, a 6 iron for example, you may find that this club is difficult for your shorter chips, due to the higher percentage of roll.

One Target with Different Clubs

From just off the edge of the green, pick a target that gives you quite a bit of room for the ball to roll. This will allow you to use more of your clubs successfully during your practice.

Rotate through each of your clubs, chipping to the same target. As you switch from club to club, be sure to play for the percentage of roll expected by choosing the appropriate landing area for each club.

Example

Start with your sand wedge and attempt to land the ball halfway to your target. Progressively rotate through your golf clubs changing your landing area appropriately.

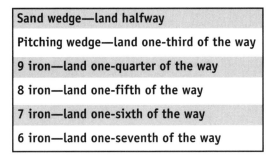

Sand wedge—land halfway

Pitching wedge—land one-third of the way

9 iron—land one-quarter of the way

8 iron—land one-fifth of the way

7 iron—land one-sixth of the way

6 iron—land one-seventh of the way

Hit a few chips with each club and then switch. Work your way up and down the club continuum to help you learn how the different clubs react, and how to correctly choose your landing target.

Once you are feeling relatively successful, change to quality-goal practice. This is an important part of your practice, as you know it will increase your on-course consistency.

A good quality goal would be to chip four balls in a row within four feet of the cup with each of your clubs. If you find this too easy, try five with each club during your next practice session.

You may find that you prefer certain clubs in this situation. This will help you with your on-course club selection.

Increase Your Goals as You Improve

To continue to improve, increase the difficulty of your goals as you accomplish them.

This is similar to the way you should increase your weights when you work out. Weights that I used to struggle with seem easy now. To continue to see improvement, I need to increase my weights. My friend Kristin recently became a certified physical trainer, and she gave me some new workouts to try. They were not that much different from what I was doing, but the variety provided me with new challenges and increased the quality of my workout time.

Increase the difficulty of your golf goals either by increasing the number of times in a row you must accomplish the task or by decreasing the acceptable distance from your target. As the quality of your practice increases, so will your on-course consistency.

My friend Jeff Warne wrote in the book *Shrink Your Handicap,* which he coauthored with Phil Lee, that if you cannot hit fourteen tee shots in a row on the driving range, it would be unrealistic to expect this on the golf course. I have since added the quality goal to my practice session to be able to hit fourteen successful tee shots in a row on the range. This has increased my driving consistency on the golf course.

Major League Pitching

A pitch is a relatively high-lofted shot where the ball travels farther in the air than it rolls on the ground. You might pitch if you need your ball to travel over an obstacle, such as long grass or a bunker, but do not want the ball to roll a lot when it lands.

Pitching requires more air time.

You will choose to pitch as your last option, when you have ruled out putting and chipping. Because a greater percentage of the shot is in the air, a larger swing is required, making pitching inherently less consistent.

Use Your Sand Wedge

You'll want to use your sand wedge for pitching because it is the most lofted club that most golfers carry. The loft will help to promote the desired travel in the air with less roll.

Bounce

Your sand wedge also has what is called bounce. And don't feel bad if you have never heard of bounce. When I tried to play golf for a living, I never understood how the bounce worked, and that it could help me.

You can see the bounce on your sand wedge by looking at the bottom, where the trailing edge is higher than the leading edge. The bounce, or trailing edge, is what should be set on the ground, so that the leading edge may be slightly off the ground. This is to your advantage as it will allow the club to skip across the ground, rather than digging in. This allows the club to react like rocks skipping across water. As long as you use the bounce, rather than the digging edge, the club head will keep going, rather than getting caught in the ground and stopping as if it had hit a brick wall. If you make a mistake and the club hits the ground early, before the ball, the club continues to slide across the grass, picking up the ball, and avoiding disaster. If you do not set the club properly and use the leading edge, you unfortunately tend to dig into the ground too much. Should you then hit the ground before the ball, the club will immediately dig in and stop, better known as the not-so-fun chili dip.

It would have helped me a lot if I had understood this concept when I was playing. I remember being paired with my good friend Kathy, when she and I were playing in the Swiss Open on the Ladies European Tour. We were playing a par 3. In our usual fashion, she missed the green to the right, and I missed to the left. We both went to hit pitch shots. She chili-dipped hers, and I skulled mine. Obviously, neither of us knew how to use the bounce of our sand wedge properly. If we had, hers would not have gotten stuck in the ground, and I would not have been so hesitant to hit the ground.

Conclusion: You will use your sand wedge for pitching because of its loft and bounce.

Pitching Setup

To Ensure Proper Use of the Bounce

Your setup for pitching is the key to successful use of the bounce. You'll want to check the following areas if you find your sand wedge digging in too much:

1. **Club sitting properly on the ground**

2. **Grip**

3. **Shaft angle**

My student Joanne sometimes struggles with the club's digging, and these are the three areas we focus on.

First, your sand wedge must be set properly on its bottom, so that the bounce rests on the ground, with the leading edge slightly off the ground. If you incorrectly set the leading edge in contact with the ground, the sharp edge will tend to dig in if you hit the ground on your swing.

Second, you will want to check the way your hands are positioned on the club. If your hands are rotated too far to the right, the club face will close, causing it to aim left at impact. A closed club face will bring the leading edge into contact with the ground, causing it to dig in. In most cases that I have seen, the right hand is the culprit. Be sure that your right hand completely covers the thumb of your left hand. Other than the thumbnail, you should not be able to see any of the fingernails of your right hand. The palm of this hand should face the target and not the sky.

Third, the shaft of your sand wedge should be relatively straight up and down, so that the butt end of the grip points toward your belly button. You want to avoid leaning the handle excessively forward, to the left, because once again this will bring the leading edge into contact with the ground and tend to make the club dig in.

Checkpoint

You think you are set up properly to use the bounce, but how do you know? You can check, without a golf ball, by taking some swings with the bottom of your club contacting a solid surface, such as a painted two-by-four. I would recommend that you start with small swings, so you don't scare yourself to death when you do contact the wood. If you are using the bounce properly, the board will leave a mark on the bounce, not the leading edge.

Fundamentals Review

A pitch shot is a miniature version of your full swing, ranging from a small swing up to nearly your full swing. The percentage of air travel is what defines it as a pitch.

Your grip and your posture will be like that of your full swing, with some adjustments in your setup to assist in distance control.

Distance Control: Being Accurate All of the Time

The size of your swing will control the distance that your pitch shot travels. The larger the swing you take, the more velocity you achieve, which propels the ball a greater distance.

Working with Mike Adams really improved my pitching, and my ability to teach it. He showed me how to use the setup to help control the size of the swing. I now use a modified version of his method in my teaching.

Your Setup Controls the Size of Your Swing

Alter your setup to help control the size of your swing by changing:

1. **Hand position on the grip of the club**

2. **Width of stance**

The smaller the distance you require, the smaller swing you should take back and through. You can produce the smaller swings through a smaller setup. This makes sense! So, for your smaller pitch shot you should place your hands all the way to the bottom of the grip of the club and narrow your stance so your feet are almost touching. When you grip down on the club, you in essence make it shorter, which generates less power and less distance. When you narrow your stance, you restrict your lower body, which will provide resistance and limits the size of the swing you'll be able to take. This will also limit distance.

The Pitching Continuum

You can use your setup to control the size of swing all the way from the smallest pitch shot to your full swing with your sand wedge. This can be as short as two yards all the way up to sixty yards, depending upon your distance ability. Use your setup as a continuum. Start from your smallest setup, with your hands all the way down to the bottom of the grip and feet completely together. Try a few pitches from this setup. Slowly increase the size of your setup by gradually placing your hands higher and slowly widening your stance. You should feel that as you increase the size of your setup, the size of your swing and the distance the ball travels increase also.

You can increase the setup size all the way to your full swing, with your hands to the top of the grip and your feet hip width apart.

Know at Least Three Pitches—Small, Medium, and Large

You will want to know at least three pitch shots, including small, medium, and large. You should be able to repeat the setup for each and know the distance that the ball travels in the air, measured in yards.

By using your setup to help you to control your swing size, you will be much more consistent with your distance control because you will not need to think excessively to limit your swing size. You will be able to just let it happen. The less you need to think during the swing, the greater your chance of success.

Small

For your smallest pitch shot you'll want to place your hands all the way to the bottom of the grip and narrow your feet so they're almost touching. If you narrow your feet to this extent and feel completely off-balance,

For your smallest pitch shots, you will want to grip down to the bottom of the handle and narrow your feet so they are almost touching. Notice that as your arms hang naturally to the center of your body, the end of the club points to your belly button.

The small pitch requires a small motion that is mostly arm swing. Notice that it is the same length back and through.

feel free to widen them slightly. For your baby, tiny pitch shots I recommend that you try placing your hands so low on the grip that your lower hand may be partially off the grip and on the shaft of the club.

This small setup will allow you to take only a small swing. This small swing will generally only be an arm swing, with minimal to no wrist hinge, due to the amount the body is restricted by the setup.

My smallest pitch shots only travel eight yards in the air. You need to know how far yours travel.

Medium

For your medium pitch shot, you'll want a medium setup, where your hands are positioned in the middle of the grip on the club and your heels are three to four inches apart. This medium setup should allow you half-swings, where your left arm travels to parallel to the ground, and your wrists have started to hinge. The amount of wrist hinge is an individual preference and should reflect what you would do at this point in your full swing. They should hinge in reaction to the club head's being heavy, rather than in a forced motion.

Keep in mind that when you pitch, your swing should be the same length back and through. Your forward swing should be the mirror image of your backswing. So as your backswing size increases, so should the length of the forward swing. Your medium pitch is a large enough swing that you will start to have some natural body rotation in reaction to the larger arm swing. This medium pitch shot is also a large enough swing that your right heel should be coming up off of the ground, at least slightly, on your forward swing, in reaction to the body's motion.

My medium pitch shot travels thirty yards in the air. How far does yours travel?

For your medium pitch shot, your hands should be in the middle of the grip and your heels three to four inches apart.

In your medium pitch shot, your arms should swing back and through to about hip level.

Large

Your large pitch shot is nearly the size of your full swing with your sand wedge. In your large setup, your hands will be to the top of the grip of your club, so you have the full length of the club to swing. Your stance should be at its full width, where your heels are no wider than shoulder width. This large setup will allow you nearly your full swing, if not full. Your left arm will travel to about ten on the clock, based upon your flexibility. Your wrists will be fully hinged at the top of your backswing in reaction to the club head's swinging. The larger arm swing will rotate your body, with your right heel coming off the ground, up to the toes, on the forward swing, in reaction to the larger motion.

My large pitch shot travels fifty-five yards in the air. How far does yours travel?

For your large pitch shot, your hands should be to the top of the grip and your heels hip width.

The large-pitch setup will allow you nearly your full swing.

Yards Measured in the Air

Your pitching yardage should be measured to where the ball lands, not adding in any of the roll. The amount of roll will vary greatly based upon where the ball lands. This will be factored in when you're choosing your landing area during your preshot routine.

Think like a Professional: A Pitching Routine That Works Under Pressure

What are the lower-handicap players thinking and doing while they prepare to hit a pitch shot? They are not just winging it. They have a checklist of tasks to accomplish in a specific order before the ball is struck. The stronger your fundamentals and your routine, the more likely your contact, direction, and distance are to be consistent.

Determine Shot Type

The first step is to determine if you have to pitch. Being a risky shot, it should be your last choice. You'll want to rule out a putt or a chip first. You will have to pitch if you have more ground to carry than green to work with and you cannot land the ball short of the green.

Determine the Landing Area

Next, to determine your landing area, consider the following:

1. Firmness of the ground

2. Speed of the greens

3. Slope of the green—uphill, downhill, or side hill

4. Position of the pin in the green

5. Trouble to avoid—bunkers or water, for example

The firmness, speed, and slope of the green will affect how much the ball rolls when it lands. The harder, faster, and more downhill the green, the sooner you will want to land the ball due to the increase roll each of these contributes. And vice versa, the softer, the slower, and the more uphill, the closer to your eventual target you will want to land the ball since these minimize the roll.

The position of the pin in the green should affect your decision as to where to land the ball, so that you always favor the fat of the green. For example, if the pin is located on the near edge of the green, giving you little room to work with, your landing target would be even with the pin. This is to avoid possibly leaving the ball short of the green and needing to pitch again. If the pin is located all the way in the back of the green, you may want to land the ball too short of the pin, to avoid hitting the ball over the green and once again needing to pitch. By playing for the side of the pin with the bulk of the green, even if you slightly miss the shot, you will more consistently end up on the green putting.

You should also consider any trouble it may be necessary to avoid. For example, you may want to aim slightly left of the pin to keep from hitting over a water hazard or a bunker.

As you can see, many factors must be considered when choosing your landing area. Do you take the time to do this? If you do not, you should start. Bob Rotella stresses the importance of a specific target. The smaller the target you choose, the more you narrow your focus, and the greater your chance for success. I recommend any of his golf books if you're looking to improve the mental side of your game.

Set Up to Produce the Necessary Size Swing

How far is it in yards from your golf ball to your chosen landing area? A yard is one big step. You may want to pace off distances occasionally during your practice sessions to improve your ability to judge distance. The necessary yardage will determine the size swing you need to take. Use your setup adjustments—where on the grip of the club you place your hands and the width of your stance—to help define the size of your swing. You should know the distance that your small, medium, and large pitch shots travel. If the needed distance is in between those of your medium and your large pitch shots, adjust your setup in between those of your medium and large. Your hands should be slightly higher on the grip of the club relative to your medium, but not as high as your large, and your feet would be slightly wider than for your medium, but not as wide as for your large. You have an infinite number of setups to assist you in distance control. The more you practice, the more accurate you will become.

Realistic Practice Swing

Set up exactly as you have determined is necessary for you to produce the desired swing size. Take a realistic practice swing or swings while looking at your landing area. The practice swing should be the same size and tempo you will take when you strike the ball. You will also want your practice swing to hit the ground, as this will be necessary to get the ball into the air. You should focus on your landing area during the practice swings to help to limit your target and to confirm visually your desired distance.

Aim, Align, and Go!

You've determined you're pitching. You've picked your landing area. You've chosen your setup. You've taken your practice swing. You have set the stage for success. Now you need to pull the trigger.

To aim your club face to your target, which is the landing area, set the scoring lines on the face perpendicular to the target line. Remember, your sand wedge should rest on the bounce.

After you aim your club face and align your body so that it generally sets parallel to your target line, you are ready. This process should not take a long time. Take one last look to your target after you complete your setup routine, then repeat exactly what you did in your practice swing, allowing the ball to just get in the way. Your setup should not be too slow or inefficient, so that the feel of your practice swing will be fresh in your mind, so that this is something you are repeating, rather than experimenting with.

If you have trouble with your aim and alignment, you may step behind the golf ball to pick an intermediate target on the ground to aim over.

Trajectory Control: Hit It High or Low and Impress Your Friends

Now the Fun Part—Use Your Imagination

You can alter your ball position to control the trajectory of your pitch shots. Not only can you control your distance through your setup, but also how high the ball travels, which would in turn affect the amount of roll.

The farther you position your ball back in your stance, the more your ball will roll. The more forward you position the ball, the more loft you will get. A more detailed explanation follows.

Right for Roll

The farther right of center you position your golf ball within your stance, the more you decrease the loft in the face. Try it! Set your sand wedge in the center of your stance to start. This will show you the actual loft in the club face, which in most cases is fifty-six degrees. While leaving your club face aiming in the same direction, slowly baby-step your body to the left, so that the club head ends up more toward the right side of your body. You should notice that the club-face angle alters, the loft progressively decreasing the farther the ball position moves back in your stance. In the shot option called the pitch and run, although the ball will travel the majority of its distance in the air, the ball will roll more than it would in a centered-ball position. This would be to your benefit if the pin is located toward the back of the green, where you could land the ball on the front edge and allow the ball to roll back.

You may also be forced into this option when your golf ball ends up in a questionable or bad lie.

The numerous possibilities for ball position let you use your imagination. Every little bit you move the ball back, the more loft you take away.

Keep in mind that as you alter your ball position, and therefore the loft, you will need to adjust your swing size. If my sand wedge's effective loft is decreased, the size of the swing necessary to produce the same distance will decrease.

Left for Loft—the Lob

Yes, the farther forward you position the ball in your stance, the more you increase the effective loft of your club. But, be careful! First, you need a good to near perfect lie. And second, this shot is higher risk because the increased loft will require you to take a larger swing to attain the same distance as from a more centered position. The larger swing tends to be less consistent.

I like to use the saying "right for roll and left for loft" when I teach, because I believe it helps my students to remember how changing ball position controls trajectory. Right for roll is a useful shot, but left for loft only when you have to.

To see how positioning your ball forward of center affects the club face, set your sand wedge in the center of your stance. While leaving the club face aimed at the same place, slowly baby-step to your right, so that the club ends up farther left relative to your body. You should see that the loft increases as the club moves farther left in your stance.

You will need a perfect lie to be successful when positioning your golf ball more forward in your stance. The slight cushion provided by the good lie helps minimize your chances of hitting the ball fat or thin, which can easily occur if the ball position is too far forward, due to the semicircular shape of the golf swing.

If you want to move the ball position slightly to increase your loft, then do so only slightly, one to two inches at the most. Second, you should only attempt to hit a true lob shot if your back is against the wall, with no other options. An example would be one down with one to go in the club championship, and the pin is located one step on the green tucked over a bunker. Then, and only then if you have previously attempted the shot in practice, should you try it.

One of the best pieces of advice I've received about the lob shot came from Mike Adams. Understand that as you move your ball position forward in your stance, your shoulders open relative to your target, aiming them more to the left. It is important that your club face continues to aim at the target when you make this adjustment. What Mike explained to me is that your arms should swing along your shoulder line. Relative to the target line, this produces an out-to-in path, and therefore a left-to-right, cut spin. A cut spin reduces speed, like a cut shot in tennis, and promotes a higher, softer shot. This is also known as the lob shot. Understanding how the arms swing along the shoulder line helped my understanding of how pitching and specifically the lob shot work.

Phil Mickelson is well-known for his ability at lob shots. He has an amazing short game, and it is fun to see how short he can hit the ball and land it softly with such a large swing.

The Sky Is the Limit

I have always enjoyed teaching pitching because the possibilities are endless. With a little imagination and a little practice, you can learn to control your distance through your setup and your trajectory through your ball position. The number of combinations is endless. The more skilled you become, the more of these options become a part of your repertoire.

Do You Need a Lob Wedge?

Rather than dealing with all of these adjustments, why not just purchase a lob wedge? I was always taught not to answer a question with a question, but here goes. For the number of lob shots that you need to hit during your round, is it worth taking a club out of your set and replacing it with a lob wedge? In most cases I do not think so. I use my 9 wood much more during my round than I ever feel I need a lob wedge. Also, if you need a lob wedge that often, it might be more productive to question your course management than to add the club.

Dave Pelz is a big advocate of the lob wedge, and if you feel it would help your scoring, then certainly do not rule one out. Before using one, be sure to practice with it to help you adjust to the needed swing size due to the increased loft in the club face.

I've never owned a lob wedge, but seeing some of the shots that players can hit with this club, I've considered it. I would not carry it in my bag full-time, but might substitute it in if I was playing a course where the greens are more elevated and firm.

Practice Techniques for Pitching Consistency

Your first goal for your pitching practice should be to work on your fundamentals and improve your solid contact.

Use a monorail system similar to that you used for putting, but this time use a soft object such as a folded towel. This will help you to check your setup and swing path. Vary your swing size, which is controlled by your setup, to hit the ball different distances. You should be checking that the bounce is properly hitting the ground, so that the club is not excessively digging in, and also that your swing is the same length back and through.

Once you are comfortable with your fundamentals and your contact, you'll want to graduate to working on your distance control, by hitting to specific targets.

Place a folded towel just outside your golf ball to check your alignment and your swing path. Your club head should never contact the towel.

The Towel Drill

Place towels at ten-yard increments, at ten, twenty, thirty, forty, and fifty yards. You can pace these yardages and set a towel at each ten-step increment.

Always remember to use your setup to control your swing size, and therefore your distance.

Using a relatively small setup, attempt to land your golf ball on the ten-yard towel. Once you feel relatively successful, move on to the twenty-yard towel. The size of your setup should increase to promote a slightly larger swing. Try to hit the twenty-yard towel with the ball as it comes out of the air. Once you feel successful at twenty yards, continue on to the towels at thirty, forty, and fifty yards.

Alternate your target with each ball. Move from ten to twenty to thirty yards and so on, then go back down. This will help you to learn to adjust your setup for different distances.

The towel drill to practice distance control.

Quality Goals

Now it is time for your quality practice, to help you increase your on-course consistency. You need to set and accomplish a quality goal before you can quit. For example, your goal may be to hit to the ten-yard towel for five out of ten balls. This may sound like a low percentage of success, but it is not as easy as it sounds, depending upon the size of your towel. Your goal may be five out of ten for the twenty-yard towel, four out of ten for the thirty-yard towel, and three out of ten for the forty-yard towel. As the distance increases, your percentage of success will decrease. You should stay at each distance until you accomplish your goal. What happens when you get to that last ball to your ten-yard towel, and you need it to hit the towel to accomplish your goal? Here is the pressure you experience on the course every day. If you can make your practice resemble your on-course experience, you are being productive. To be more consistent on the golf course, you must be accountable for the quality of practice as well.

My friend Terri came to visit me in Bridgehampton one summer. We had some free time and decided to practice. We placed a wire range basket about fifteen yards from us. Our goal was to each have two golf balls land and stay in the basket. I had a little bit of an advantage because I practice this quite regularly and it was the practice area where I teach every day during the summer. It took me about eight to ten minutes to accomplish my goal of two balls in the basket. Terri took a little longer, however—approximately one hour. I admired her perseverance. But those who know Terri would expect nothing less.

Same Target—Vary Your Ball Position

Pick a target to pitch toward, at a distance of twenty to thirty yards preferably. Start with your sand wedge with the ball centered in your stance. Hit several shots to your target. The more your landing area resembles a regular green, the more beneficial. Once you're having success, start to slowly move your ball position back in your stance to hit varying degrees of pitch and runs. This will help you to learn to adjust your swing size to offset the decreased loft as a result of the ball position. Continue to alter your ball position, but now back toward the center, then slowly move your ball position left of center to hit varying lob shots. Be aware of the necessary adjustment to your swing size to accommodate the increased loft as a result of the forward ball position.

Now, set your quality goal. For example, you may want to hit three balls from very different ball positions—forward, center, and back—in a row within five feet of your target. This will require you to successfully adjust your swing size under the same pressure you experience on the golf course every day. You may find it helpful to run through your routine during your practice just as you would on the golf course.

Quality practice goals will help to increase your on-course consistency. They should also help with your shot selection, as you may find that one of the three ball positions brings you to your target more consistently than the others. Vary your target and distance with each practice session.

Full Swing: Being Efficient and Consistent

5

Your full golf swing is simply a slightly larger version of your pitch shot. This is why practicing your pitching is beneficial to your full swing.

Solid Fundamentals

Your setup fundamentals are so incredibly important in shaping your golf swing. Your grip, ball position, posture, aim, and alignment set the stage for a successful swing.

Concepts to Understand

- Your grip controls your club face.

- As a result, your grip can cause you to alter your swing path.

- **Your posture affects balance and therefore solidness of contact.**

The preswing fundamentals mentioned above are your building blocks. This is the biggest difference between handicap groups. The lower the handicap, the more you'll see consistency in that player's setup. Many of the golf lessons that I give involve fixing the student's setup, which directly affects the golf swing.

For example, what if a player has too much knee flex, with her rear end tucking under as a result and all of her weight on her heels? That player would be off-balance—off-balance toward her heels, so that she would appear to stand up during her golf swing and probably top the ball. The untrained eye, better known as Prince Charming, would probably give her the bad advice to stay down or keep her head down. But a trained professional would fix the posture, and therefore the balance, and now you have solid contact and a happy camper again! To solve the problem, fix the most basic fundamental that is being violated.

Assuming that your preswing fundamentals are relatively solid, let's talk about the swinging motion.

Natural Is Good

In my opinion, too many golfers are tied up into position golf, rather than respecting the natural athletic motion that occurs when you simply swing your arms and allow your body to react.

Start with the Arms Swing

To understand how your swing starts, we will start with the bottom half. Practice swinging your arms back and through continuously from hip level to hip level. Although your body will react naturally to the motion, no large or forced motions are necessary. Your shoulders will move slightly, but are not yet being pulled excessively to turn.

You should notice that as your arms swing back, your right arm slightly folds at the elbow. The elbow should also point down to the ground. As you swing your arms forward, your left elbow should fold, so it also points down.

If you are having trouble with your full swing, you can always go back to some half-arm swings.

The advantage to understanding that your golf swing starts with an arms swing is that the golf club will correctly stay in front of your body. If you incorrectly start your golf swing by turning your entire body, the golf club will end up trapped behind you, in need of inefficient rerouting to get the club face back to the ball.

Backswing

The Turn Is a Result

You hear about it on TV. You read about it in the golf magazines. You hear the announcer comment on how Tiger has such a wonderful turn, and that is why he hits it so far. And it sure would be nice to hit it as far as Tiger. Not likely, but fun to imagine. Students come to me so concerned with their turn that half the time they're screwing themselves into the ground, and losing the natural athleticism they possess. As I mentioned earlier, if you turn too early, your golf club will incorrectly get sucked in behind your body and will need rerouting to get back to the golf ball. So, understand that your golf swing starts with the arms swinging.

As your arms swing back to start your golf swing, your left underarm should swing across your chest. As you continue to swing your arms back, with your left underarm connected to your chest and the width of your arm swing, this will pull your body to turn. Your body's rotation is a result of the swing width and the left underarm connection. By allowing this rotation to be a natural result, you are more likely to repeat it under pressure.

The connection of the left underarm and the width of your golf swing will allow your swing to be centered and rotary. Your body is rotating around your spine, so that in your backswing your shoulders turn ninety degrees away from the target. As you turn around your spine, the bulk of your upper body moves to your right side and produces a natural weight transfer onto a solid right foot.

Right Arm Pulls the Left Arm Wide
Your right arm will fold on your backswing, so that the elbow points down. The folding of the elbow elevates the golf club. Although your right elbow folds, it should never bend past ninety

To practice your backswing, grab your left wrist with your right hand and practice the necessary width to pull your shoulders to turn.

degrees. You can practice this by grabbing your left wrist with your right hand. Allow your right arm to pull your left arm wide as you swing your arms back. This will establish the necessary width for your golf swing. But, be sure to allow your left underarm to stay connected to your chest. Once again, you should notice your body rotating as a result of the connected width. You can practice this with or without your golf club. If your golf club feels too heavy, place your left hand low on the grip of your club.

One of my students, Cynthia, always had an excessively long backswing because she allowed her right elbow to bend past ninety degrees. Once she added to practice sessions this drill of allowing her right arm to pull her left arm wide, the length of her backswing improved dramatically and so did her ball contact.

This drill will also help you determine the proper length for your backswing. I like to see the left arm swing to about ten on the clock. This will vary slightly from person to person based upon flexibility. You'll want to swing your arms back with width to the point where your body resists. Your right arm pulling your left arm wide, and not bending past ninety degrees, will help to determine the proper swing length.

If you overswing, your right elbow will bend beyond ninety degrees, and in many cases you may incorrectly feel yourself stand up and come out of your posture. Your weight may also then incorrectly move forward toward your left foot on your backswing.

Your arms should travel to approximately ten o'clock.

Wrists Cock and Hinge in Reaction to the Swinging Club Head
The club head of a golf club is heavy relative to the rest of the club. As you swing the club back with momentum, your wrists should react naturally to the weight in the club head. This natural hinging of the wrists will make the club head feel lighter as the club forms the letter *L* with your left arm. For this to happen naturally, your grip pressure must not be excessive. In other words, avoid the death grip. Your fingers should be closed around the club, but not excessively squeezing. Try to be relaxed enough so that you can feel the weight in the club head.

Backswing Summary

1. Swing starts with arms swing.

2. Left underarm should stay connected to the chest.

3. Right arm pulls left arm wide to establish width.

4. The centered, rotary motion turns the shoulders ninety degrees as weight transfers naturally to the right foot.

5. Right arm should never fold past ninety degrees.

6. Grip pressure should be soft enough so the wrists react to the swinging club head.

7. Connection and width pull the body to turn as a result.

Forward Swing

Your forward swing is very much a result of your backswing. You have stored energy through the elevating of the club and the coiling of the body.

The motion of your forward swing should be athletic, similar to when you throw a ball or make a tennis swing. I prefer it to be as natural, and as much of a reaction, as possible. The more natural a reaction the motion is, the easier it is to be consistent. To understand what should happen is good, but to overthink or play position downswing is not.

The Arms Do the Down, the Body Does the Around
As your arms swing down toward the ground, your right arm unfolds to maintain width. This width will be necessary for your club to hit the ground, and the ball to travel into the air. To help you feel the proper direction for your arms to swing down, the left underarm should maintain its position against your chest.

A complete, balanced finish position. Note the position of the right foot.

As your right arm straightens and your arms swing down, your body should rotate toward the target to face forward. This rotation is a natural uncoiling of the body toward the target.

As your body turns forward to face the target, your trailing foot should rotate up onto the toes in reaction to the body motion. Your right knee will turn to face the target and should finish relatively close to the knee of your left leg, once again like throwing a ball. This will finish the centered and rotary motion of your golf swing as your body rotates around to the left side of your spine and produces a natural weight transfer onto your left foot.

The Left Arm

After the right arm straightens and your arms are fully extended, the left arm will start to fold, and the left elbow should point down to the ground. This straightening of the right arm and folding of the left arm squares the club face, which should produce a straighter, more solid golf shot. As your left elbow folds, your right arm will also pass over the top of your left to help square the club face for impact.

You can help yourself to feel this by grabbing your right wrist with your left hand. From your address position, swing your arms forward to the finish of your golf swing. You should feel the left elbow folding and pointing down, and the reestablishment of width in your right arm.

Balance

Not only should you be able to hold a balanced finish position, but you should be balanced throughout your golf swing. Your address position should be balanced and athletic. You should be in balance throughout your backswing. A stable lower body and good posture will assist in this. For this reason, I generally like to see the left heel stay on or close to the ground during the back-

To practice your forward swing, grab your right wrist with your left hand. Swing your arms forward to your finish position.

swing. Be balanced and athletic on your forward swing, and practice holding your finish until the ball lands to promote good balance.

Tempo

The tempo of a golf swing will vary somewhat based upon the individual. Personal life tempo will definitely affect how you swing the club.

My friend Jerry, from metropolitan New York, lives his life and swings his golf club at a furious tempo. Although we have attempted to smooth his swing down to a slow blur, he is a fine golfer and must swing within his personality—fast!

Continuous Arms-Swing Drill
A wonderful drill to help you feel tempo and arms swing is a continuous arms-swing drill. Place your feet together and continuously swing your club back and through. There should be no pausing or stopping as the club moves back and through. As you swing your arms back, be sure to keep your left underarm against your chest, so your shoulders are pulled to turn.

For the continuous arm-swing drill, place your feet together and practice swinging your arms back and through continuously.

The continuous motion will teach you balance and will force your body and swing to be efficient. If your posture or your swing is inefficient, you will find it difficult to keep the club continually swinging.

This drill can also be helpful to you on the golf course. If you are struggling with your balance, and therefore your contact, try this several times to help get you back on track.

Forward Swing Summary

1. The forward swing is a result of the backswing.

2. It should be a natural athletic motion.

3. The right elbow straightens as the arms swing down.

4. Your body naturally rotates forward to face the target, as your trailing foot rotates up onto the toes in reaction.

5. The centered rotation naturally transfers your weight to your left foot.

6. Your left elbow folds and points down to the ground to square the club face.

7. You should be able to hold a balanced finish position.

Keep It Simple

The key to your full-swing success is the solidness and consistency of your preswing fundamentals, including grip, ball position, posture, aim, and alignment.

Once you set up properly, make it natural and swing. Swing your arms, while keeping your left underarm across your chest, and let your body react athletically.

The more sports that you play, obviously the greater your field of reference for feeling athletic motion. But this can be taught and learned, provided you have a solid setup.

Sand Play
Made Easy

6

Greenside Bunker

A greenside bunker is a sand-filled area around the edges of the putting green.

You will need to determine how far you can hit a greenside bunker shot taking sand. And no, it does not count if you skull it. I would estimate that the average woman only hits her maximum-blasting bunker shot ten to fifteen yards. You need to determine this because, when you have greater than this distance to your target, you will need to attempt a fairway bunker shot. We will cover that later.

Would you be happy if you could get the ball out of the bunker and onto the green most of the time? I've seen it all in the bunker. I spent a year teaching bunker play, roasting in the sun at PGA National, and learned a lot after seeing some interesting styles.

I love teaching greenside bunker play because it is not nearly as difficult as most women think it is. It isn't magic, it's just keeping it simple and realistic.

The two basic problems I see are being way too fancy, and trying to hit bunker shots as Tiger Woods would, or your husband or significant other who thinks he's Tiger.

Throw the Sand Out

You must understand that if you can consistently throw the sand out of the bunker, the ball will consistently come with it. The club should never touch the golf ball, but throw the sand and the ball with it.

The splash setup: hands to the top of the grip, ball position left of center, and feet dug in.

Setup and Fundamentals Review

Set Up Properly to Take Sand

Your setup will determine your ability to throw the sand out of the bunker. So, stop thinking that you are good enough to hit that spot two inches behind the golf ball over and over, as everyone incorrectly keeps telling you. Start setting up properly so the sand just gets in the way.

1. Hands to the Top of the Grip on Your Sand Wedge

You'll want to keep your hands to the top of the grip on your sand wedge. This maximizes the length on your club and helps you to take sand.

If you grip down on the club, you effectively make the club shorter and make it harder to take sand.

2. Position Ball Left of Center

You'll want to position your golf ball left of the center of your stance. I like to see the golf ball just left of your left cheek. Here, the ball is left of where the club would naturally hit the ground and enter the sand.

If you position the ball to the center or right of center in your stance, you will likely strike the ball before the sand. This is not good or fun! If this happens, the ball may not get into the air enough, so it may hit the lip and possibly not emerge from the bunker, or possibly go flying across the green.

3. Dig Your Feet In

You'll want to dig your feet into the sand to lower yourself to help you to take sand. If you do not dig your feet in, the bottom of your swing will be higher, and it will be more difficult for you to splash the sand.

Everything you've done with your setup to this point is to help you to take sand. Take some practice swings, without golf balls, and see that you can and do take the sand. If you are not taking sand, check all three setup provisions and keep swinging until you can consistently splash the sand out of the bunker.

Forget Everything You've Been Told and Swing

Forget all the fancy-schmancy bunker advice you've heard and take your normal full golf swing and splash the sand out. The ball should travel out with the sand. Yes, your normal full golf swing, where your trailing foot (right)

For your splash shot, throw the sand out of the bunker and be sure to go to a full finish.

comes up onto the toes in reaction to your body's turning forward to face the target.

I know it feels strange to take such a full swing so close to your target, but the sand acts as a buffer between the club and the ball, which keeps it from flying too far. One of my students, Sara, has a beautiful golf swing, but it took nearly an infomercial on my part to convince her to take a full swing for her greenside bunker shots. Ever since she convinced herself to take a full swing, she has been fantastic out of the bunker.

If It Works, Keep Doing It!

If you feel that you are a good bunker player, and you have your own style, absolutely keep doing it. If it is not broken, do not try to fix it. But if you struggle, as many women I have watched seem to, go back to the simple bunker style with no bells and whistles. Once you can get the ball out of the bunker, then and only then should you worry about trying to get the ball close to your target.

If the Sand Feels Heavy or Your Sand Wedge Seems to Be Digging In Too Much

If your sand wedge feels as if it is digging in too much or getting stuck in the sand, you should first double-check that you are taking a just-like-your-7-wood full swing.

If you are taking a full swing and your sand wedge still feels as if it is getting stuck, you should check your club face at address. It is important that your sand wedge is set properly on its bottom, so that the bottom, better known as the bounce, can glide through the sand.

If you incorrectly hood your sand wedge, which will aim the face to the left and take loft away from the face, the sharp leading edge will tend to dig in and get stuck as it enters the sand. This is a common mistake I see. The face can look too flat or unbalanced when it is set properly. If you try to make the loft of your sand wedge look like the loft of your pitching wedge, digging in is the obstacle you will face.

When your sand wedge is set correctly, the writing on the shaft of the club will usually be on the top. And there is generally a mark on the grip of the club, sometimes very small, that shows you the center of the grip. The writing should be on the top of the grip, not rotated to the left. This is assuming that the grips on your clubs are on straight.

Out of the Bunker and onto the Green Summary

1. Splash the sand and the ball will come out with it.

2. Your setup helps you to take sand: hands to the top of the grip, ball positioned to left of center, feet dug in.

3. Set your sand wedge properly—flat on its bottom.

4. Forget all you've been told and take your full, regular golf swing.

Consistent Bunker Play

If you wish to be consistent in getting out of the bunker, you must be able to throw out sand. So practice simply that. Practice taking full swings and throwing sand out of the bunker and onto the green.

Quality Goals

Your quality goal may be to take fourteen swings in a row where you splash the sand onto the green. If your twelfth swing does not splash the sand, you should start over again at one. This will help to put the pressure on your practice that you experience every day on the golf course.

This is a wonderful way to practice because you learn to swing the club and the sand just gets in the way. This will help you avoid the dreaded chop and stop that you often see from the sand.

Once you are successful in simply throwing the sand out of the bunker consistently, add a golf ball. The goal should remain the same. Throw the sand out, and the ball will come with it. Now, set a quality goal with the golf ball. Your goal may be to hit five balls in a row out of the bunker and onto the green. The fifth ball will have the pressure you experience every day on the golf course. If this goal is too easy, increase the number of balls in a row or require them to be within a certain distance of your target.

Do You Need to Get Fancy?

You've heard all the advice before, but not from me. Generally, it is unnecessary and bad, including that you need to open the club face, you need to open your body, you need to pick the club up steeper, you need to feel as if you're cutting across the ball. But you did not hear it from me. The reason being that, for 85 to 90 percent of the women I teach, this advice would be hurtful. Too fancy, and too many adjustments can lead to bunker play disaster.

So how do you determine if you're in that 10 to 15 percent who need to make some adjustments in your setup?

Answer one simple question: When you hit a bunker shot, splashing sand, does it travel farther than you need or want?

If your answer to this question is no, or if you have trouble hitting your bunker shots far enough, stop right here. You do not need to ever get fancy. Stay with the simple setup mentioned previously, and stick to your normal full swing. So 85 to 90 percent of you should stop reading about the splash shot right here and move on to the next section.

For the 10 to 15 percent of you who answer, yes, when you

take sand, the golf ball travels farther than you need or want, you should make two slight adjustments in your setup.

For a shorter bunker shot, open your club face more by rotating the grip of the club to the right, then placing your hands on the grip. When you rotate the grip to the right, you open the club face and increase the loft. A more lofted club will produce a higher, therefore shorter, shot. You'll still need to take a full swing. When you open the club face, the club face will aim more up, but it will also aim more to the right. You will need to walk your body around to the right to aim the club face more to the left—in other words, back to your target. Be careful that as you aim your body more to the left to realign the club face that you walk around a semicircle to the right to maintain your ball position left of center.

The degree to which you open the club face will vary the distance you hit your sand shots. The more you open the face, the more you increase the loft, and the smaller the distance the ball will travel.

When you open your club face to hit a shorter splash shot, you will need to walk your feet around the imaginary semicircle (pictured here with golf balls) to realign the club face to the target.

Short Bunker Shot Summary

1. Open your club face more by rotating the grip of the club to the right, then placing your hands on the club.

2. Aim your body to the left by walking around a semicircle to the right to realign the club face to the target.

To Splash or Not to Splash?

When should you take sand, and when not? The distance of the shot decides. But, the first question you need to answer is, how far can you hit the ball when you splash sand? The maximum distance that you can hit the ball when you splash sand will determine when you need to switch from the blast shot to a fairway bunker shot. When you hit a fairway bunker shot, you will not take sand. I would say the maximum splash shot for most women ranges between ten and twenty yards, depending upon strength and swing speed. Let's say your maximum splash shot is twenty yards. Anytime you need to hit the ball from the bunker more than twenty yards, provided that the lie of the ball is good enough, you will hit a fairway bunker shot.

Fairway Bunker Shot

You've determined that you need the distance of a fairway bunker shot, but first you need to assess the lie to see that it is good enough to allow you to use this shot. Generally, the ball will need to be sitting on top of the sand, or at least in a position where you can comfortably get the bottom of the club below the bottom of the ball. If the lie is not good enough, or the ball is sitting down in the sand, you may have to sacrifice the distance and just play for a splash shot out.

Setup and Fundamentals Review

Narrow Your Stance and Grip Down

By narrowing your stance, you stand taller, which makes it less likely you'll contact the sand. This will also eliminate some lower-body motion. By eliminating lower-body motion, you'll stay more centered and make it easier to contact the ball before the sand.

When you grip down, you effectively shorten the club, making it less likely that you will take too much sand.

Experiment with each of these to find the right amount of each you need to catch the ball cleanly, without sand, coming out of the bunker.

If you are still taking too much sand, you may also wish to move the ball slightly farther back in your stance to promote catching the ball before the sand.

Club Selection

When choosing your club for your fairway bunker shot, the first thing to consider is the height of the lip of the bunker your golf ball needs to go over. You can get a pretty good sense of how high your ball will travel with each iron by setting the club on the ground and stepping on the club face. Be sure to do this outside the bunker to avoid the "rules shark" from getting you. The angle of the shaft, pointing up, will show you the

For a fairway bunker shot, narrow your stance and grip down on the club.

approximate angle that the ball will come off the club face. Your first priority must be to choose the club with enough loft to clear the lip that the ball must go over.

The second thing to consider is the distance the ball needs to travel. You should take one to two extra clubs, to offset the distance you'll lose through the setup changes, provided the height of the lip allows this. The ball will travel less coming out of a fairway bunker, but you can compensate for this by taking extra club.

Take Your Normal Golf Swing

Once you set up, you will want to forget you are in the sand and take your normal golf swing. You have made the necessary adjustments through your setup and should not attempt to alter your swing in any way.

If you are at a distance where a full swing would not be necessary from off the grass, take that smaller-than-full swing.

You can get a pretty good feel for the trajectory of the ball off an iron by setting the club flat on the ground and stepping on its face.

Can You Use Your Fairway Woods?

A 9 wood or a 7 wood can work nicely out of a fairway bunker. I would avoid the lower-lofted fairway woods, such as the 3, unless you have a perfect lie and there is a reward for your risk. If by taking this risk you might reach the green, rather than being short, it might be worth it.

Fairway Bunker Summary

1. Assess the lie to determine that a fairway bunker shot is possible.

2. Choose your club based upon the height of the lip and the distance to the target.

3. Grip down.

4. Narrow your stance.

5. Position your golf ball slightly back in your stance.

6. Take your normal golf swing.

Buried Bunker Lie: Look Like a Magician

You walked up to your golf ball and found the dreaded fried egg: The golf ball is buried in its own pitch mark. It looks bad, but with a few setup changes, you can successfully get the ball out of this precarious-looking position.

The Breakers Resort, where I am thrilled to be teaching in the winters with some wonderful instructors and friends, recently totally redid their ocean course. In an amazing transformation, the course is unbelievably improved. One of the very qualified instructors, Mark Hackett, and I played the course the day before it was officially scheduled to reopen, so as to be familiar with its rerouting. I was definitely in my fair share of the ninety new bunkers. On the tenth hole, my tee shot buried in the lip of a fairway bunker so much that I could only see a small speck of the ball. A little depressing, because I knew I could no longer get to the green on my next shot, but with the proper setup I could at least get the ball out of the bunker. Getting the golf ball out is your first priority when the ball is buried. It is not as hard as it looks.

For a buried bunker lie, position your ball right of center and allow your weight to favor your left foot throughout the swing.

Setup and Fundamentals Review

Position Your Golf Ball Slightly Back in Your Stance

Placing your golf ball slightly back in your stance will slightly deloft your club face. This will bring the digging edge, the leading

For a buried bunker lie, swing steeply down and into the sand with momentum.

edge, into contact with the sand and help dig the golf ball out of the hole.

Your Weight Favors Your Left Side

Your weight should favor your left side at your setup and throughout your swing. When your weight favors your left foot, it will tilt your shoulders, so that your left shoulder is lower than normal, making your angle of attack steeper. The steeper angle of attack helps the club to dig through the sand and extract the ball.

Swing Down into the Sand with Momentum

Your setup with your weight on your left will make your swing steeper to help extract the ball from the sand. To understand how this works, understand what causes a tee shot to pop up excessively. The angle the club approaches the golf ball is the angle at which the ball comes off the club. A buried ball will come out of the bunker because of the steepness of the club into the sand, produced through the setup. Once you've completed your backswing—and a full one will be necessary to generate enough momentum—you'll want to swing the club down and into the sand. The angle of attack and the momentum of the club into the sand will extract the ball. The resistance of the sand may inhibit your ability to follow through. This is absolutely fine, but do not allow yourself to anticipate this and slow down your swing. Your club head should have momentum as it enters the sand.

Buried Bunker Lie Summary

1. Play your golf ball slightly back in your stance to activate the digging edge.

2. Your weight favors your left.

3. Take a full backswing and swing your club head down and into the sand with momentum.

4. The goal is to get the ball out of the bunker: recovery.

Increasing Your Distance

7

Wouldn't it be fun to hit the golf ball like Tiger Woods? Just once, I would love to feel what that is like. I say that, but if I did it once, I would certainly want to be able to do this over and over.

Human nature: No matter how far you do hit the ball, you'll always want to hit it farther. So how do you hit the ball farther?

Solid Fundamentals

The more solid your fundamentals and the more efficient your golf swing, the longer your ball will travel. The first answer is easy. The better your grip, the more square the club face will be at impact. The more balanced your setup, the more speed you'll be able to generate due to increased efficiency.

Practice Techniques for Increased Distance

You must learn how to swing your club head to generate more speed. Here are several drills to increase your club head speed.

Swoosh the Grip

Everything is relative. You can better feel the weight in your club head when you compare it to the weight of the grip end. Turn your club upside down and place your hands on the shaft just below the club head. While doing this, maintain your regular golf posture so that the end of the grip is not near the ground. Swing the club and relax your wrists and forearms enough so that the grip makes a swooshing noise at the bottom of your swing. Any unnecessary squeezing or tension in your hands and arms will make this difficult.

Speed-increasing swoosh-the-grip drill.

How loudly can you swoosh the grip? It should not take a lot of effort, but relaxing your wrists and forearms will allow you to generate more speed and more noise.

Now, turn the club over the normal way and swoosh the club head using the same motion and effort that you used with the club upside down. The club should still make the noise, but now you should definitely be able to feel the weight in the club head. The club head is heavy relative to the grip end, and this drill should make it much easier to feel.

If at any time during your golf round you feel your grip pressure getting too tight, so that you are unable to feel the club head, I recommend this drill to help speed along your recovery.

Try this drill both with your feet together and with your feet apart. Placing your feet together helps limit excessive body motion and helps you to feel your arms swing to generate the speed.

L-to-L Drill

The L-to-L drill also helps you to feel the club head swing. You can do this drill with the golf ball. With your feet together, and the ball on a tee, using a short iron, such as an 8 iron, take half-swings. As

The L-to-L drill.

you swing the club back, the shaft of the club and your left forearm, which is parallel to the ground, should form the letter *L*. As you swing your club through, with the golf ball hopefully getting in the way, the shaft of the club and your right forearm, which is parallel to the ground, should form a reverse *L*. Once again, your wrists and forearms must be relaxed enough so that your hands and arms can react to the weight in the club head as it swings.

This drill also makes the club feel lighter through your being relaxed and natural, which makes it easier to be consistent. My fellow PGA professional and friend Shani Roth and I have used this drill for a lot of our ladies' groups to help them to generate more distance.

Split-Hand Drill

You can do the split-hand drill with or without a golf ball. In either case, it will help you to feel the club head swing and will train your arms to square the club face properly in the forward swing.

Place your hands on the grip of the club and split them apart. The farther apart you place them, the more exaggerated the feel. You can place your hands anywhere from one to about six inches apart. If you are doing this with a golf ball, it will be easier if the hands are split no more than one to two inches.

As you swing your club forward, you should feel the swinging club head and how the right arm passes over top of the left arm as the left elbow folds. This squares the club face, which should help prevent your hitting the ball too far right.

I find this drill especially helpful for the natural lefties who are playing right-handed. Because their left side is so strong, the left arm tends to be too tight, not passive enough to allow the right arm to pass, causing their ball to slice.

The split-hand drill also helps to increase swing speed and distance.

"It Felt as if I Didn't Even Hit the Ball." Why This Works

As you learn to swing your club head so your swing speed increases, probably with less effort, your feeling of your ball coming off the club head may change. It should feel better. You may even feel as if you barely hit the ball, even though it went flying. When you hit the ball well, it feels so easy. Why is this?

What happens when your golf ball contacts your club face? It actually flattens or compresses against the club face, then springs off. This is just what a basketball does when it bounces off the ground. The harder you bounce the ball, the more it flattens and the higher it bounces in response.

The more speed the club head generates, the more the golf ball flattens against the club face, and the quicker and the farther the ball rebounds off the face. This is why contact feels so light and easy when the ball is correctly hit.

And conversely, this is why it can feel so bad when the ball is incorrectly hit. If the golf ball is minimally compressed, it will not spring off your club. It will more likely feel as if you hit a rock.

Proper fundamentals, and increasing your swing speed through the drills mentioned, will increase your number of great shots that feel like nothing.

Should You Be Teeing Off with a Driver?

Should you tee off with a driver, or with one of your fairway woods? Keep in mind this may change from day to day.

The driver tends to be your least consistent club, since it is the longest and has the least amount of loft. The lesser loft will produce less backspin and therefore more sidespin. So, any curving of your golf ball will be magnified when using your driver.

Ask yourself the following three questions to determine if you should be using your driver.

1. Do I generate enough club head speed to get the ball into the air with the driver?

You must generate a certain amount of club head speed to produce adequate air time with your driver. If you hit the ball with your driver and it makes a good sound, but only flies head high, you should be teeing off with a club with more loft, such as a 5 wood.

My student Phyllis, after four years of working on her swing speed, was finally successful with the driver this past summer. It was exciting to both of us. She felt that she had really come into her own with her golf, and I found it wonderfully rewarding to see her success.

2. Am I swinging well enough today that I can hit my golf ball into the fairway?

Some days your golf ball will fly straighter than others. We all experience this. On the days the golf ball is not going where you want, tee off with a more lofted club. I remember playing in a pro-am in Montauk, New York, with Mary, Donna, Colleen, and Pat from Southampton Golf Club. I was hitting the ball so off-line it was scary. After two crooked drivers, I switched to my 3 wood on the third tee. After two crooked 3 woods, I switched to my 5 wood on the fifth tee. After two crooked 5 woods, I switched to a 7 wood on the seventh tee. And last but not least, after two more slightly off-line tee shots, I finished the round tee-ing off with my 9 wood. Yes, my ball flew shorter, but I could at least find the ball to finish the round.

3. Is the golf hole I am playing wide enough to accept a driver?

You should have a feel for your margin of error with your driver. When your ball travels off-line, how far off-line? If the golf hole is more narrow than your margin for error, consider a more lofted club to minimize your mistakes. A more lofted club will produce more consistently solid on-line shots.

Using Your Driver Successfully

1. *Check for proper ball position.* Check that your ball is in line with the instep of your left foot or your left shoulder socket. This will assist you in catching the ball slightly on the upswing to maximize driving distance.

2. *Check your shoulders so that your right shoulder is lower than your left at address.* Your right shoulder should set slightly lower than your left simply because your right hand is lower on the grip of the club than your left. This

will also help you to catch the ball slightly on the upswing.

3. *Practice swings should lightly sweep the grass with no divot please.* Your practice swing for your driver, or any wood from off a tee, should either lightly sweep the grass or not hit the ground at all. This will help to promote a sweeping angle of attack. If your club hits the ground hard, taking a divot, this angle of approach is too steep and you will lose distance because the ball is traveling too high.

The Target:
It Isn't the
Ball Anymore!

8

When you first started to play golf, your goal was to make contact with the ball. And then your goal probably became to hit the ball into the air. In both these cases, the golf ball was probably your target.

Hopefully, at this point you can accomplish airborne and forward somewhat regularly. Through applying the proper fundamentals, routines, and decision-making mentioned earlier, you are now seeing much more consistency. Now, your target should shift from the ball to the actual target. The actual target may be the center of the fairway, the center of the green, or the flag on the green.

Being aware of your target is important as it will greatly affect your setup. As you watch a better player set up for a shot, notice how often he or she looked at the target. This assists not only with aim and alignment, but also with recognition of distance.

I often see players of lesser experience going through their entire setup without ever looking up at their target. It is difficult to aim at something if you never look at it.

I can easily tell the difference between my students who still think of their golf ball as their target and those who have advanced to realizing that the target is where they wish the ball to travel to. If the student is still ball-bound, and I ask her to aim more to the left, she will often step to her left, which would incorrectly aim her more to the right. A golfer who is aware of the target will be quicker to realize that she needs to step more to her right to aim more to the left. Do you do this?

As you become a more advanced player, I suggest you look more often at your target during your setup. Watch the golfers on television. They look at their target continually throughout their setup. This makes it easier for them to position their club head as well as their body relative to the target.

Successful
Fairway Woods

9

The ironic part of women's golf is that the shot you will need to hit the most, the fairway wood, is the one that requires the most precision and solid swing fundamentals. Due to the length of golf holes, most women must play a high percentage of fairway woods.

When you learn to swing the golf club, you generally start with irons from the tee, then woods from the tee, then possibly irons from the ground. Last, you learn to hit your woods from the ground. This is in the order of difficulty, so as to give you positive results and feedback.

Since the woods are physically longer, and the margin for error when the ball rests on the ground is smaller, it takes longer to feel proficient with the fairway woods.

I grew up in western New York, where the fairways were cut long and fluffy. This made fairway woods easier. When I went to college, where the fairways were cut shorter, I struggled with my fairway woods as I adjusted.

Here are a few suggestions to help you become a more consistent fairway wood player.

Check Your Setup for Success

Your ball position for your fairway wood should be left of center, but not as far left as for a wood from a tee. This should place your ball just barely left of your left cheek.

You can also check this when you take your practice swings. Take several practice swings with your fairway woods to see where your club sweeps the grass in your stance. This will show you where you should position your ball.

If you are playing a round of golf where you keep hitting the ground before the ball, put the ball there. This may not be solving the cause of the problem, but it can certainly help you to survive the round, with your sanity and a respectable score.

Practice Techniques to Increase Consistency

Practice-Swing Drill

How many practice swings in a row can you sweep the grass? Actually try this. It sounds easier than it is. Set a goal of ten practice swings in a row that sweep the grass.

One of my new students, Joan, was having trouble with her fairway woods. I asked her how many swings in a row she could sweep the grass. She looked at me as if I were crazy and this was way too basic for her. After around fifty practice swings, her greatest total was three in a row that swept the grass. After two weeks of Joan's trying to sweep the grass consecutively, her fairway woods became much more consistent.

Start Simple and Work Your Way Up

Starting your round of golf with success can do wonders for your confidence. For that reason, I recommend your first few fairway wood shots be taken with a more manageable club, one that is shorter in length, such as a 7 wood for example. After you have several good 7 woods under your belt, graduate to a longer wood for more distance. Make yourself earn your longer fairway woods to help establish confidence early in your round. By starting with a more lofted fairway wood you will also experience more consistent contact.

Two-Tee, No-Tee Drill

This drill will help you to be more consistent in hitting your woods, or any other club, from the ground.

Place a tee in the ground with no golf ball on it. Next to that, place a tee in the ground with a ball on top. Next to that, place a ball on the ground, in a good lie. You will take three swings, starting with the empty tee. When you swing, you should clip the tee. Once you have done this, clip the tee out with the ball on top. This should

The two-tee, no-tee drill to improve your fairway woods.

produce an airborne shot. When you have successfully clipped out both tees, you should hit the ball from off the ground. It may help if you visualize a tee underneath the ball.

This progression will teach you the necessity of getting the club down to the ground to get the ball into the air. You should repeat this drill until you feel comfortable with hitting the ball from the ground.

Bringing Your Range Game to the Golf Course

Developing your preshot routines during practice and putting them into play on the course will help you achieve higher consistency. This coupled with your quality-goals practice should lower your scores and hopefully increase your enjoyment.

Here are some other techniques in decision-making to help you to have fun—yes, fun—rounds of golf.

Constant Adjustment Throughout the Round

Every round of golf requires constant adjustment. You will need to adjust based upon the course, the weather, and your level of play that day.

Adjusting to the Course

You need to adjust your game based upon the golf course that you are playing. There are numerous considerations. The more different courses you play, the quicker you will be able to adjust. Possible adjustments include:

1. The Tee Shot

Is the course wide enough for your margin of error on your tee shots? The more narrow the course, the more lofted the club you'll want to tee off with. For example, if the course has a lot of water or it is tree-lined, you may need to tee off with a 3 wood or a 5 wood.

You may experience this when you play golf in Florida or the South, where there are often numerous water hazards. When our college golf team would travel from South Carolina to Florida, it always took some time to adjust to seeing so much water and to return to focusing on the short grass. My friend Kristin and I had a ritual we called "sacrificing balls to the water gods" when we played courses with a lot of water. We would toss several golf balls into the water to satisfy the golf gods, so they would not take them when they counted toward a score. If we believed this worked, maybe it did.

2. Fairway Woods

The tighter the golf course or the shorter the fairways are cut, the more lofted the fairway wood that you will want to use.

At Atlantic Golf Club, where I teach in the summer, the fairways are cut very short. Therefore, many of the women wisely use their 7 woods for the majority of their fairway shots. The shorter club and added loft makes this more difficult situation more manageable.

3. Smaller Greens Surrounded by Bunkers or Water

The less accepting the greens, the more you should consider playing short. You should play to a distance from the green where you
are comfortable.

I played a Futures Tour event at Forsgate Country Club in
New Jersey. The bunkers surrounding the greens were so incredibly deep that you could not see the flag from inside them. In my
practice round, I decided that unless I had a 6 iron or less to the
green, I was going to lay up. During the tournament I stuck to
my game plan, and I avoided a lot of the frustration I watched
other players experience.

4. Firm or Soft Greens

The firmer the greens, the more you'll need to land the ball either
short of the pin, or in some cases short of the green, to allow for
the increased roll. This is oftentimes difficult to judge until you
experience the ball approaching the green a couple of times.

After I graduated from Furman University, my friend Kathy
Hart and I traveled to play the Ladies European Tour. Our first
tournament was in Düsseldorf, Germany. The first round of the
tournament was quite a learning experience. On the front nine, I
would land the ball on the green and it would go flying way over
the back. I shot a disappointing 43 on my front nine. On the back
nine, I made an adjustment. Whatever club I thought I should hit,
I subtracted two and hit that club. If I thought I needed a 7 iron, I
would hit a 9 iron. My adjustment worked quite well. I shot 33
and was much happier.

The reverse would be true if the course is wet or the greens
soft. You may need to hit an extra club or two to compensate for
the lack of roll.

5. Fast or Slow Greens

Greens can vary drastically from course to course. Thus it is important to spend time on the practice green prior to your round. However, sometimes this is not possible.

To adjust to fast greens, pick a spot short of the cup and aim for that, and grip lower on your putter. By picking a spot short of the cup, you can trick your eyes into seeing a shorter putt and therefore make a smaller stroke. By gripping down on your putter, you make the lever shorter, which will exert less force.

Slow greens seem to baffle people. To adjust, pick a spot past the cup to aim at and force yourself to make a larger backstroke. By choosing a spot past the cup, you can trick your eyes into seeing a longer putt, which should help to persuade you into making a larger stroke. If this does not produce enough distance, you must convince yourself to make an even larger backstroke. This will help you to store more energy.

Mother Nature Adds Variety: Weather

The weather is ever changing and will greatly affect your game plan.

Our coach at Furman, Mic Potter, always had our team out playing in the worst of weather. I remember playing a qualifying round where it was sleeting for the last three holes. My score was so high that I needed a calculator to add it up. I resorted to punching 5 irons down the center of the fairway because I could not feel my hands. This was not fun, but every tournament that our team played where the weather was inclement, we won.

Some of the more obvious weather factors you'll have to deal with are rain, wind, and cold.

Rain

The first step in preparing for rain is to have the proper gear. You'll need a decent rain suit, an umbrella, a golf bag that will not soak through, a cover for your bag, several towels, and several golf gloves. There are all-weather gloves, and gloves made specifically for rain, which work better when they are wet.

The next step and most important step is to have a good attitude. When it rains, most golfers, especially women, give up. If you can keep a positive attitude, you will already have defeated most of the field.

Adjustments for rain include:

1. Tee Off with a More Lofted Wood

As the fairways get wet, you'll receive less roll and maybe no roll at all. Consider using a more lofted wood to tee off with to increase the amount of distance the ball travels in the air.

2. Fairway Woods

For the same reason that you tee off with a more lofted wood, it may be to your advantage to use a more lofted wood for your fairway shots. As the fairways turn into a sponge, your 7 wood may be more advantageous than your 3 wood because it will keep the ball in the air longer.

3. Short Game—Use a More Lofted Club and Land the Ball Closer to Your Target

As the greens get wet, the ball will roll less, and definitely less predictably. Rather than hitting a lower, running chip, you may wish to take a more lofted club, such as your sand wedge, and attempt to land the ball close to the target.

I remember playing in the Philip Morris instructional pro-am at PGA National. It rained so hard it was amazing. I was playing with two great ladies from Minnesota. They did not want to quit, and I was already so wet, it did not matter anymore. So we kept on playing. We arrived at our last hole and the green was basically a pond. They both tried to putt the ball across the green. As soon as the ball hit the water, it would stop dead only a few steps from where we'd started. I ran to the cart and grabbed my sand wedge and pitched the ball into the air, rather than trying to roll it there. We could have spent all day trying to putt and not ever have gotten there due to the water.

4. Putting

As the greens get wet, they will get slower. Try to roll your putts past the cup to compensate.

Wind

The wind is a constant consideration for golfers. You can often tell where a golfer learned to play golf by his swing and his ball trajectory. For example, Lee Trevino learned to hit the ball low while growing up in windy Texas.

I grew up playing in little wind, and as a result I hit the ball quite high. Now I live on Long Island and in Florida, two windy locations. I did not change my swing, because my habits are too ingrained, but I did have to learn to hit a specialty knockdown shot for windy days.

My father and I took a wonderful trip to Ireland shortly after he sold his business and retired. We were relatively lucky with the weather, until the last day. We were playing Ballybunion, a truly amazing golf course. It was so windy that at times it was hard to stand. To communicate, we had to stand right next to each other and yell. My little knockdown shot came in handy that day.

Adjustments for the wind include:

1. Control Your Ball Flight, Learn the Knockdown

If it is windy, golf can often feel like a job. You must learn to hit a knockdown shot to keep control of your ball flight on your approach shots into the green. To hit the knockdown:

Take extra club: Depending upon the severity of the wind, you'll want to take extra club for your approach shot. For example, you may hit a 7 iron from your normal 9 iron distance.

Position the ball slightly back in your stance: When you position your ball slightly back in your stance, or more toward your right foot, you effectively decrease the loft in the club face. This will produce a lower ball flight. This will help to keep the wind from overaffecting your ball.

Slightly open your stance: When you position your golf ball back in your stance, you must open your stance. When you open your stance, you will pull your forward foot slightly back, where you may feel that the line through your toes aims to the left of your target. This will help to realign your shoulders and help you to square the club face at impact.

2. Take Your Medicine and Grind
Playing in the wind can be challenging and difficult. You must remember that everyone else is playing under the same conditions. Some golf holes will play so much longer that they will require an extra shot or two. If this is the case, just take your medicine and grind extra hard for when you can save strokes through your short game.

To hit a knockdown shot, move the ball back and slightly open your stance.

Cold
Other than being smart and canceling your tee time when the mercury drops, there are adjustments to be made.

Consider a ladies' golf ball: The cold weather will make it more difficult to compress the golf ball. This will decrease your overall distance. By choosing a ladies' golf ball, which requires less speed to compress, it will be easier for you to compress your golf ball and help to minimize the distance lost.

Take extra club: Even though you've chosen a lower-compression ladies' ball, you may still need to take extra club. This will help to offset the lost distance.

Adjusting to Your Game That Day

The longer you play golf, the more you realize the game is fickle. What works perfectly on one day may not work at all the next. For this reason, you will want to adjust your game plan to match your game. You should adjust not only day to day, but within the same round. Your ability to adjust your game plan to match your game that day or at that particular moment will directly affect your consistency.

The Good

You warm up on the driving range, and surprise, surprise, you are hitting the ball solidly and exactly where you want.

This green light will allow you to be more aggressive during your round. You can tee off with your driver, or the least-lofted club that you normally use. You can hit your lower-lofted fairway woods to gain extra distance. This will be the day you are more likely to aim for the pin tucked over the bunker, or to go for the green over the water, rather than playing around it.

In a perfect world, you would hit the ball perfectly the entire round, but that's not realistic. You'll need to adjust your club selection or aggressiveness. If at any time during the round your ball-striking quality decreases, you will benefit by choosing clubs that are easier to hit (shorter and more lofted, generally) to help you to get back on track. Once your confidence returns, you may return to your original, more aggressive game plan.

The Regular

Your average round of golf will probably include drifting in and out of solid ball striking. This is where adjusting is the most important. You should be willing to adjust down to easier clubs to hit if you are struggling or feeling your confidence decrease. If your 3 wood from the fairway leaves something to be desired, adjust down to a 5 or 7 wood to help you regain your confidence.

Earn your longer, more aggressive clubs by having success with the easier clubs first. For example, on the first hole you might tee off with your 3 wood. This club is easier to hit than your driver and will hopefully set a good tone for the rest of the round. After your 3 wood is successful from the first tee, you can graduate to your driver on the second hole, provided the situation warrants this. On your first fairway wood shot, it often helps your confidence if you use a more lofted fairway wood, such as a 7 wood. When that is successful, you can graduate to a longer fairway wood to gain distance.

This continual adjustment will help you to keep your score down and your confidence up.

The Ugly

You've just warmed up on the range, and it wasn't fun. Contact seemed to be optional, and when you did make solid contact, the direction was as consistent as rolling dice. You need to adjust your normal game plan, and quick. If you stick with your game plan, and the club selection from when you are hitting the ball well, you may experience the not-so-fun "golfer's meltdown." You need to find a club, however short it may be, with which you can hit. It may be your 6 iron. A 6 iron eighty yards down the fairway is better than a 5 wood sliced out of bounds.

On-Course Swing Adjustments—Know Your Tendencies

Do you know your swing well enough to be able to self-correct on the golf course?

The longer you play, the more you should be able to recognize your mistakes. This is also something you should work on with your instructor. I feel this is one of my most important jobs with my more advanced students. They must be able to recognize the signs that tell them that they are starting to return to one of their old bad habits.

My student Nancy will start to hit the ball slightly to the right when her arms start to get too tight. She needs to recognize the sign of the slight fade when it starts, before it turns into a big slice. This is when I start asking her questions. She must be able to recognize this early enough to avoid a serious problem and have the know-how to get herself back on track midround.

You've just swung your 7 iron, and your ball scooted along the ground and dead to the right. Not the shot you imagined, that is for sure. Where did you hit it on your club face, off the toe or in the hosel? You need to know, because the corrections for each can be polar opposites. Off the toe, and you may be standing too far from the ball. Off the hosel, you may be too close. Total opposite corrections for two totally differently missed shots that can look similar. For this problem, you could quickly check by placing a head cover just outside your golf ball. (This would not be legal in a tournament on the course.) When you swing a 7 iron and hit the head cover with your club head, you know that your miss was probably in the hosel.

As mentioned earlier, this is something you should absolutely be working on with your professional. You must be able to recognize the signs of your bad habits creeping back in before they become major. To do so, learn to recognize where on your club face you are miss-hitting the ball.

I used to watch *Oprah* quite a bit. One of Oprah's perspectives that I really liked was to recognize the little pebble in your shoe before it causes a blister. This is a good metaphor for golf. You need to recognize the little problems before they become big. This is also a good metaphor for life. It has helped me with mine.

Play for Your Hook or Slice

Rather than trying to fix the problem on the course, you can just adjust for the direction that the ball is curving. If you are slicing, aim left enough to accommodate the curving. If you are hooking, aim right enough to keep the ball in play. This may be enough to help you get through the round, until you have time to get to the range or to your professional.

However, be sure to attend to your ball-flight problem before it compounds. Understand that if you hook the ball and you aim more to the right, over time your hook will increase. The opposite will be true if you are slicing the ball and you aim more to the left to compensate; over time your slice will increase.

Be Conservative—Play Around the Trouble

Play around the trouble to the path of least resistance when your ball striking is lacking. This is the last day you should be aggressive and go for it. Take the conservative, chicken route. It may take that extra shot to get there, but it will help to avoid the dreaded X on the hole.

Characteristics of a Successful Golfer

11

To improve your golf requires patience, focus, and persistence.

I am patient. If I were not, I could probably not do my job as I do. Part of why I believe I am this way is because I have spent a large part of my life playing golf. I know the patience and hard work it takes to improve.

It will be difficult for you to recognize your improvement day to day. You must compare over a longer time, such as month to month, or year to year.

My student/friend Cheryl always comments how much better she thinks she should be. I am quick to remind her of how much she has improved year to year. She is now accomplishing tasks on the golf course that she only dreamed of a year or so ago. For this reason, I recommend you look at the big picture to avoid the day-to-day emotional roller coaster the game can provide.

The ability to focus on the task at hand is a characteristic of a successful golfer. Try to do seven or eight things at the same time, and you will often find that you are unable to do a good job with any of them. This is what will happen if you attempt to work on too many changes in your swing at the same time. Or if you choose to listen to every little piece of advice, you'll experience the same frustration. I experienced this after college when I attempted to play golf, work part-time in the golf business, and work part-time for a money manager to utilize my college degree. I found I was not very successful at any of these because I was spread out too thin. The money management was quickly ruled out because I was miserable being indoors on nice days. A few too many wayward golf shots eventually ruled out the playing. And now I love my job teaching, and I feel I can be successful pretty much every day.

This single-minded focus is what you should apply to your golf and your practice.

What are you working on to improve your golf? I hope it is not too many more than one or two things. Identify your largest fault, and be successful with changing this. Then you can move on to the next goal.

If you are working on strengthening (rotating more to the right) your left-hand grip to keep you from slicing, and you hook the ball as a result, this is okay. It is okay. The focus is to not slice, remember! To criticize the hook is to undermine the success in getting rid of the slice. Do you do this to yourself? Many, many students do! You are trying to keep from topping the ball and hit one fat. This is okay. The opposite mistake is okay.

As instructors, we often teach using opposites. If you hook the ball, I would obviously want more slice characteristics so as to straighten your ball flight.

Focus on the task at hand. Succeed, and then you can move on. Persistence will be rewarded. In my opinion, this is the difference between those who succeed with their golf and those who do not. My roommate in college, Margaret, was a respectable player, but no better than I. She now plays on the LPGA tour and has won a couple of events. Golf was her sole focus, and she worked hard on her game until she succeeded. I give her a lot of credit.

A great example of how persistence pays off is the level of golf at Atlantic Golf Club, where I teach during the summer. The members are not only supernice people, but very successful in life. They know the benefit of persistence and hard work. They have applied this intensity to their golf game. The first summer I was there, the range was actually a dangerous place to be. So many errant shots were flying all over, you really needed to keep your eyes open. Seven years later, it still amazes me how much the level of play has improved. Hard work, focus, patience, persistence, and some respectable instruction, I and the other instructors would hope, added to their improvement.

Another example of persistence I learned from one member at Atlantic. Dr. Charles Kelman, a respected eye surgeon, gave me a copy of his autobiography, *Through My Eyes*. In his life, things hadn't always gone as planned. Failure after failure were overcome by persistence, allowing Dr. Kelman to achieve great things. His persistence increased many people's quality of life, and I thank him for the lessons I have learned from him. Although I have given him golf lessons, I am sure I have learned more from him than he from me.

Conclusion

You Can Be the Golfer You Dream Of!

Consistency on the course is a result of solid fundamentals, proper decision-making, routine, and productive practice time.

Apply the fundamentals, routines, and practice techniques described in this book over time. Your commitment to a plan for your golf will be rewarded with the greater consistency you desire. Give yourself a specified time to commit to these techniques, three to six months for example, then assess your progress. Your increased consistency will be directly proportional to your level of commitment and your focus on these ideas. I am sure that the techniques mentioned here will help to improve your golf game.

Part of the magic of golf is that you can always continue to learn. The longer you play, the better you get to know yourself and your game. I learn new things every day.

Some of the greatest life lessons I have learned came from my father, my family, my friends, and my golf. I hope you enjoy the game of golf and that it increases your quality of life. It is a wonderful way to spend time with family and friends. But, remember, it is a game! Enjoy!

Glossary

Part of becoming a true golfer is sounding like a golfer. Your lingo alone can define your level of ability. Listen to other golfers speak, and have your professional help you with this as well.

Address: The way you position your body in relation to the club and to the ball.

Aim: The position you set your club face to control the initial direction of the ball.

Aim spot: A spot you will pick on the putting green to compensate for undulations, or a spot where you will land the ball when it comes out of the air for your short game or full swing.

Alignment: The position in which you set your body to control the direction of the ball.

Alignment aid: Either a club or a device, usually placed on the ground, used in practice to help you to aim and align properly.

Away: The person who is "away" is farthest from the target and will be the first to play the next shot.

Balata: A soft material for golf ball covering that helps lower handicapped players in an effort to get the ball to stop rolling quicker.

Best ball: A tournament where a determined number of the best score of the team on each hole counts as the score for the team. For example, one best ball of two or two best balls of four.

Birdie: Scoring one shot less than par on an individual hole.

Bite: When the ball stops rolling quickly.

Blading: Hitting high on the ball, causing it to go low and run rather than get into the air. Also called hitting the ball thin, skulling, or topping the ball.

Bogey: One stroke more than par on an individual hole.

Bounce: A characteristic of a sand wedge where the trailing edge is higher than the leading edge, allowing the club to glide across the ground or sand rather than digging in.

Break: The curving of the ball on the putting surface caused by undulations.

Bunker: A sand- or grass-filled indentation in the ground.

Chili dip: Hitting the ground before the ball, normally causing the ball to go a shorter distance than planned. Also called chunk, fat, or hitting behind the ball.

Chip: A shot of relatively short distance, hit with little wrist movement, in an effort to get the ball onto the putting surface as close to the hole as possible.

Chip and run: A chip hit with a less lofted club or more in line with the back foot, producing a less lofted shot with more roll.

Chunk: Hitting the ground before the ball, normally causing the ball to go a shorter distance than planned. Also called fat, hitting behind the ball, or chili dip.

Closed face: The club face aiming left of the intended target line in relation to the line of your feet.

Closed stance: Body or line of feet aiming to the right of the target rather than parallel to target line. Stomach faces away from the target more.

Course rating: A number computed based upon the difficulty of the course, necessary to figure out handicap.

Cup: The plastic lining in the putting green where the flagstick is inserted.

Cut shot: A small curvature of the ball from left to right for a right-handed player. A small slice. Also called a fade.

Divot: A chunk of turf removed from the ground with the club head in a swing.

Dogleg: A severe change in direction to the right or left on a hole.

Draw: A small curvature of the ball from right to left for a right-handed player. A small hook.

Drive: The first shot hit from each teeing ground.

Driver: The 1 wood.

Duck hook: A very severe curvature from right to left of the ball for a right-handed player. A large hook.

Eagle: Two strokes less than par on an individual hole. For example, a one on a par 3, a two on a par 4, or a three on a par 5.

Fade: A small curvature of the ball from left to right for a right-handed player. Also called a cut shot.

Fairway: The closely mown area between the teeing area and the putting surface.

Fairway bunker: A bunker greater than approximately 30 yards away from the green.

Fat: Hitting the ground before the ball, normally causing the ball to go a shorter distance than anticipated. Also called a chunk, hitting behind the ball, or chili dip.

Flagstick: The flag and pin placed into the cup or hole on the putting surface of each hole. Also called the pin.

Fore: What you should yell if your ball is heading where it could possibly hit another person.

Foursome: Most commonly a group of four players, normally the maximum number of players allowed to play together.

Fried egg: A ball buried in the sand of a bunker.

Fringe: The slightly longer cut of grass surrounding the putting surface. Also called the apron.

"Gimme" or a putt that is "good": A short putt conceded by an opponent. Not legal in stroke play.

Green: The closely mown surface that contains the cup and flagstick. Also called the putting surface.

Green side bunker: A sand area surrounding the green or putting surface.

Greens fee: The amount charged to play a golf course. Often does not include the cart charge.

Gross score: The actual shot on a hole or round before handicap is subtracted.

Handicap: The number of strokes you can subtract from your gross or total score, computed by taking a percentage of your best scores. The handicapping of the holes is a ranking of the holes in order of difficulty, ranging from 1 to 18. The handicap system allows players of different abilities to compete on an equal basis.

Handicap index: A traveling handicap that allows you to plug your number into the course chart to convert your handicap to an appropriate handicap for that course.

Hazard: A yellow- or red-staked area, including sand bunkers.

Hitting behind the ball: Hitting the ground before the ball, normally causing the ball to go a shorter distance than planned. Also called chunk, fat, or chili dip.

Hitting the ball thin: Hitting high on the ball, causing it to go low and run rather than get into the air. Also called blading, a skull, or topping the ball.

Honor: The player with the "honor" is the person who has the right to tee off first on the next hole by scoring best on the last hole. If there is a tie, the order remains as it was on the previous hole. If you are playing ready golf, this is sometimes ignored.

Hook: A severe curvature of the ball from right to left for a right-handed player, left to right for a left-handed player.

Knock down shot: A specialty shot designed to hit the ball lower to control ball flight. Generally used in windy conditions.

Lag putt: A putt intended to just get the ball close to the hole.

Lateral hazard: An area marked with red stakes or lines.

Left hand low: A putting style where the hands are reversed so that the left hand is lower than the right to assist in maintaining wrist angles throughout your putting stroke.

Lie: The position in which the ball sits on the ground.

Lip: The front edge of the bunker.

Lob shot: A specialty shot with either a sand wedge or a lob wedge designed to hit the ball very high so that it will not roll a lot when it lands.

Lob wedge: A wedge with a lot of loft, usually 60 degrees, designed specifically to hit the ball very high.

Loft: The angle upward of the club face. Also the height or trajectory of a shot.

Match play: A competition between two players or teams decided by the team winning the most holes, each hole worth only one point.

Medal play: A competition based on the player with the fewest total strokes winning. Also called stroke play.

Mulligan: A second try after an unsuccessful attempt. Not legal.

Net score: Gross or actual score minus your handicap.

Open face: A club face aiming to the right of the intended target line.

Open stance: The line of the feet aiming to the left of the target for a right-handed player. Stomach faces more toward target.

Out-of-bounds: An area marked with white stakes from which you are not allowed to play the ball, penalty being stroke and distance.

Par: The score an expert golfer is expected to make on a hole under normal conditions allowing two putts.

Pin: The flag and pin placed into the cup or hole on the putting surface of each hole. Also called the flagstick.

Pitch: A lofted shot, smaller than a full swing, intended to get the ball up and close to the pin. Bigger than a chip and smaller than a full swing.

Pitching wedge: A 10 iron.

Plugged ball: A ball embedded in the ground.

Pop-up: A tee shot that travels too high and short, usually caused by the angle of attack being excessively steep.

Preferred lies: Rules that when in effect allow players to lift, clean, and place the ball within a predetermined length from where the ball lies no closer to the hole, provided the ball originally lies in the fairway of the hole you are playing. Also called winter rules.

Provisional ball: An extra ball hit from the original area where the ball lay, in an effort to save time, in case the ball originally hit is lost or out-of-bounds.

Pull: A shot that goes left of the target line with no curvature for a right-handed player.

Push: A shot that goes right of the target line with no curvature for a right-handed player.

Putting: The rolling of the ball in an effort to get the ball into the cup with a club designed with little or no loft.

Putting surface: The closely mown surface that contains the cup and flagstick. Also called the green.

Quality goals: A goal set with a specific percentage of success in mind to help you to increase your consistency on the course.

Rough: The area to the sides of the fairway, with longer grass.

Sand wedge: An 11 iron, a club with a lot of loft. Hits ball high with less roll.

Scramble tournament: A team tournament in which all players teeing off choose the best shot and then hit from there. This process continues until the ball is holed, including putts.

Scratch golfer: A golfer with a zero handicap.

Setup routine: A specific order of placing the club to the ball and yourself to the club enabling you to find the proper distance from the golf ball in a balanced athletic position.

Setup station: Placing clubs on the ground, two parallel in a railroad design and one perpendicular, to help you to set up properly with your aim, alignment, and ball position.

Shank: A shot hit out of the neck or hosel of the club, causing the ball to go severely right and often low.

Shotgun start: The method by which groups start on different holes at the same time, therefore finishing at the same time.

Skull: Hitting high on the ball, causing it to go low and run rather than get into the air. Also called blading or hitting the ball thin, or topping the ball.

Sky: To hit the ball extremely high, causing a loss in distance. Noun: pop-up.

Slice: A ball curving severely from left to right for a right-handed player.

Slope: A number based upon the difficulty of the golf course, necessary to compute handicap. Different for each set of tees.

Spikes: Golf shoes.

Splash shot: A bunker shot, generally short in distance, hit from around the edge of the green, where you will throw the sand out and the ball will come with it.

Stroke play: A competition based on the player with the fewest total strokes winning. Also called medal play.

Strong grip: Positioning the hands onto the club where they are rotated more to the right than they hang naturally, often producing a ball that travels to the left.

Surilyn: A hard material used to cover a golf ball recommended for new players promoting distance and durability.

Swoosh: A noise you want the grip of the club in a drill, or the club head, to make indicating swing speed maximizing distance.

Take-away: The first two feet of the club moving away from the ball initially.

Target line: An imaginary line extended through the ball to the target.

Tee: The peg on which the ball is placed for the first shot of each hole. Also the area from which you hit your first shot of each hole.

Tee shot: The first shot on each hole.

Tee time: A time assigned at which you may play the course.

Tempo: The pace of the swing.

Threesome: Three players in a group.

Topping the ball: Hitting high on the ball, causing it to go low and run rather than get into the air. Also called blading, a skull, or hitting the ball thin.

Twosome: Two players in a group.

Unplayable lie: A position in which the ball sits where the player opts to take a penalty stroke in order to move the position of the ball within two club lengths no closer to the hole.

Up and down: Taking one chip and one putt to get the ball into the hole.

Weak grip: Positioning the hands onto the club where they are rotated more to the left than they hang naturally, often producing a ball that travels to the right.

Whiff: To swing and miss the ball completely. Not the end of the world.

Winter rules: Rules that when in effect allow players to lift, clean, and place the ball within a predetermined length from where the ball lies no closer to the hole, provided the ball originally lies in the fairway of the hole you are playing. Also called preferredlies.

You've managed to develop a respectable game, now learn how to lower your score

FROM THE AUTHOR OF
THE WOMEN'S GUIDE TO GOLF AND
THE WOMEN'S GUIDE TO CONSISTENT GOLF

Kellie Stenzel

PGA MEMBER AND
TEACHING PROFESSIONAL

THE WOMEN'S GUIDE TO LOWER SCORES

The essential guide to making the
shots that can reduce stroke count
and improve your overall score.

THOMAS DUNNE BOOKS

St. Martin's Press